ALSO BY NAOMI LEVY

To Begin Again: The Journey Toward Comfort, Strength, and Faith in Difficult Times

Talking to God

TALKING TO GOD

Personal Prayers for Times of
Joy, Sadness, Struggle, and Celebration

Naomi Levy

DOUBLEDAY

New York   London   Toronto   Sydney   Auckland

PUBLISHED BY DOUBLEDAY
a division of Random House, Inc.

DOUBLEDAY and the portrayal of an anchor with a dolphin are registered trademarks of Random House, Inc.

A hardcover edition of this book was published in 2002 by Alfred A. Knopf.

The Library of Congress has cataloged the Knopf hardcover edition as follows:

Levy, Naomi.
Talking to God : personal prayers for times of joy, sadness, struggle, and celebration / Naomi Levy.— 1st ed.
p.   cm.
1. Prayers.   I. Title.

BV245 .L46 2002
291.4'33—dc21
2002025498

ISBN 0-385-51003-9

PRINTED IN THE UNITED STATES OF AMERICA

November 2003

7   9   10   8   6

for Rob, Adin, and Noa
the answers to my prayers

Contents

Contents

Contents

Contents

Contents

Acknowledgments

Many thanks to my agent, Esther Newberg, who is a trusted advisor and advocate. Peter Gethers inspires, encourages, and points the way. What more can you ask from an editor? And thanks to Leyla Aker for all her indispensable input and help.

William Goldman is my writing rabbi. He guided me patiently through periods of writer's block and insecurity, and taught me to believe that my words could help others. Ed Solomon made it possible for me to seek out the best agent and publisher. Daniel Adler believed in this work from the start and offered his unique assistance.

The following dear friends and colleagues read this manuscript and left their invaluable imprint upon it: Rabbi Elliot Dorff, Rabbi Laura Geller, Rabbi Susan Grossman, Rabbi Eli Herscher, Dr. Joseph C. Hough Jr., Rabbi Richard Levy, Teresa Strasser, Carol Taubman, Rabbi Burton L. Visotzky, Rabbi Stewart Vogel, and Father Michael Wakefield. I am deeply indebted to them all for their wisdom and sage counsel.

Rabbi Michele Sullum, Jacob Sullum, and Francine Allen Sullum are inspirations to me. I thank them for allowing me to share their story. Rabbi Mark Borovitz provided his insight on the subject of addiction. I received many blessings from our family's two religious communities, Temple Mishkon Tephilo and Temple Beth Am.

Thanks to Dr. Helene Rosenzwieg, Andrea and Warren Kay, and to all my friends too numerous to name who heard me out, held my hand, and brainstormed with me.

My father, George Levy, of blessed memory, taught me how to pray. I would sit beside him at *shul* playing with the fringes of his *tallis* and listen in as he talked to God. Although it has been twenty-four years since my father died, his love continues to fill me with strength, courage, and faith.

My mother, Ruth Levy, strengthens me when I feel weak, calms me when I panic, comforts me when I am sad, advises me when I am confused, and encourages me always. Her wisdom and love sustain me.

My mother and siblings—Dr. Miriam Levy, Dr. Daniel Levy, and David Levy—read my words with great care and offered me their sound and loving advice.

My in-laws, Sari and Aaron Eshman, have given me their love, reassurance, and support. My sisters- and brothers-in-law, nieces and nephews, aunts, uncles, and cousins have all been sources of help and joy.

My husband, Robert Eshman, blesses all my days. His influence on this book is everywhere. He has given me his ear, his criticism, his keen editorial eye, his constant encouragement, his wisdom, his patience in reading my manuscript more times than he would care to remember, and his love.

My son, Adin Joseph, and my daughter, Noa Rakia, are my sweet blessings, my inspiration, my light, and my comfort.

Whole and complete, this work is my prayer to God, Creator of all.

Introduction

Talking to God

I like to sit in houses of worship long after the worshipers have gone. All alone in the dark, way up in the balcony or in the last seat of a cavernous hall, I sometimes find myself imagining words that have passed from the congregants' whispering lips to God's ear. Prayers seem to hover in the air like the smell of a fire long after the flames have died out. These prayers are not the ones that come from books. They are less literate, without rhyme or meter, without fancy embellishment. The ones not printed in black and white, but in all the subtlety and mystery of the human soul. They are prayers of life and death, joy and mourning, longing and thanksgiving. Prayers shouted in anger or sung out in love. They are daily prayers, once-in-a-lifetime prayers. Prayers of women and men, of the healthy and the ailing, of the young and the elderly, of the rich and the poor.

Canonized prayers contain ancient and eternal wisdom and are central to religious experience. They are dependable and beautifully written. Often set to sublime music, they link us to our community when we recite them together, and to our history when we remember that these very words were uttered centuries ago. They connect us to future generations as well, for they will continue to inspire for centuries to come. No matter what our religious tradition, established prayers are the framework of our faith. We teach them to our children and turn to them again and again throughout the measure of our days. They instruct us in the articles of our belief, in our unique bond with God, and in the particular expressions of that relationship.

But what are we to do when the prayer book does not contain the words we are searching for? What do we do when certain feelings well up inside us, but the words to express them are absent from our liturgies?

I first started writing my own prayers when I was pregnant with my son. Pregnancy is a miraculous experience, and there was so much I wanted to say to God. I wanted to give thanks; I wanted to tell God about my worries, my hopes, my awful morning sickness. I wanted to pray for the health of my child. So I found myself talking to God each day, and soon I was writing down new prayer after prayer. And I have never stopped. The process of writing these prayers became a source of enormous joy and comfort. It helped calm my fears as I approached labor and delivery. I could talk to God in plain English, without any pretense. I could enter into an intimate relationship with God.

At the moment when I gave birth I handed my obstetrician a handwritten prayer and asked him to recite it over me, my husband, and our newborn child. At first he looked at me as if I were nuts, but then he started reading, and suddenly he began to cry. Later, he said he'd never had such a spiritual experience in his life.

Prayer writing became so natural for me that when I wrote my first book, *To Begin Again,* I instinctively concluded each chapter with a prayer. After I finished the manuscript, however, I contemplated removing the prayers. I worried over them until just before the publication date. The prayers were certainly helpful to me, but I feared readers might reject them, even laugh at them. Now I am so glad I chose to leave these prayers in because I have been completely overwhelmed by the response to them. A Catholic priest told me he keeps the prayers at his bedside. A psychologist who leads a support group for incest survivors ends each session with one of the prayers from *To Begin Again.* A rabbi told me that when he arrived at a cemetery to officiate at a funeral, the mourners handed him one of the prayers I had written to recite at the service. A young woman told me that she had gone to see her doctor because she was suffering from feelings of sadness and grief. She had hoped he would prescribe Prozac. The woman smiled and showed the prescription note to me. Her doctor had instructed her to read the prayers in my book.

People of all faiths have complained to me that many of their traditional prayers do not always move them. They say the flowery language and the formality of the prayers are an obstacle to their spiritual expression. I have often felt the same way too. Certain prayers leave me feeling empty.

Some people are shocked when I encourage them to supplement their traditional prayers with personal, spontaneous ones. They assume that making any change to the prayer service is forbidden. But they are mistaken. Composing personal prayers is not a sin, it's a blessing. It is a way to restore our communication with God. Where do you think all the prayers in the prayer book came from? They weren't written in heaven. They were created by human beings who were filled with awe and who wanted to share their thoughts and feelings with God. Religious expression is not some relic from the past. We should never hesitate to give voice to our souls.

"Pray for me, Rabbi" is probably the most common request I hear from those who come to see me. My response is always, "Of course I will, but I need your help." And I encourage the person seated before me to tell me what he or she wants me to say to God. Inevitably, the most heartfelt and beautiful words of prayer issue forth from the very mouth that had previously been unable to pray. Stunned and proud, the individual returns to the world blessed with the gift of personal prayer.

It is remarkable to see what can emerge from us when we stop trying to pray to God and start *talking* to God instead. Too often we envision prayer as something saintly and proper. Something that has strict rules and standards. We get intimidated and inhibited. But talking to God is a very natural and intimate experience. We can talk to God anywhere: in the shower, in the car, at work, in bed. We don't need to sound smart or polished. We don't need to ask anyone else to do it for us.

I have spent the last nine years writing my own prayers and teaching others how to talk to God as well. Wherever I go, whenever I teach or lecture or visit the sick, I ask people to take a moment, listen to their hearts without censoring, and speak to God. Some speak their prayers aloud, some write them down on paper, others pray silently in their souls. What emerges is overwhelming. A young mother who lost her daughter to gun violence asked God to watch over her precious baby. An old man told God how he'd like to be welcomed on the day of his death. A breast cancer survivor thanked God for her health and added that she viewed her cancer as a gift that taught her how to treasure each day of her life. A lonely ten-year-old boy asked God to help him make up with his best friend. A woman in her forties turned to God to help her rekindle her marriage. A respected surgeon prayed to God for the power to heal.

But talking to God doesn't always come easily. Talking to God implies that there is a Being who cares and understands, and, even more than that, one who helps and heals. There are times when we need and want to talk, but we fear that God isn't listening. Sometimes we are too angry with God to begin a conversation. Sometimes we do talk, wait for a reply, but receive no answer. So we walk away feeling hurt and abandoned. There is nothing more humiliating than pouring out your soul to someone who isn't paying attention. What's the point of that, we ask ourselves.

You might think that I, a rabbi, spend my days in blissful devotion to God. But prayer doesn't always come easily to me either. Yes, there are times when my heart opens up to God all by itself in a flurry of passion. But there are other times when my heart feels like a stone—heavy, hard, and silent. There are times when God's presence seems as near to me as my own breath. And there are other times when God's very existence seems like a mere concept—lifeless and uncertain.

I intended to begin writing this book three years ago. I discussed it with my editor and publisher, and they were very enthusiastic. They sent me a contract, and I was about to sign it. Then life intervened.

I gave birth to our daughter in 1996. She was beautiful and perfect, and we named her Noa. In Hebrew, Noa means "motion" or "movement," and we thought the name suited her perfectly because she was always on the move inside me. Noa is also the name of a very powerful female character in the Bible. In the Book of Numbers, she and her sisters confront Moses about an unfair law that discriminates against women. Moses is so flabbergasted by their courageous appeal that he isn't sure how to respond. He turns to God and asks God what to do. God replies, "These daughters are correct." Noa and her sisters manage to change the law. They teach Moses a way to deal justly with women.

When our Noa was two, we began to realize there was something the matter with her. Ironically, it had to do with her movement. Her muscles were weak and undeveloped, and her balance was off. She would walk and fall over, then get up and stagger around. At first, we refused to believe there was any problem. We'd watch her fall and tell ourselves she was just a late bloomer, she'd grow out of it. But over time Noa's difficulties were undeniable. Especially when I'd get those looks of pity from the other moms at the park. It was then that we started taking her from doctor to doctor, hoping someone would tell us she was just fine, or that there was a simple cure to her disability. We saw orthopedists, neurologists, geneticists, cardiologists, and developmentalists. They ordered scores of blood tests, a brain MRI, DNA tests, an EEG, and an EKG. Some doctors were optimistic and told us Noa would continue to grow stronger. Others frightened us by raising the prospect of harrowing degenerative diseases. Some doctors were kind and compassionate; others were cold and aloof.

I couldn't believe this was happening to my daughter. It all seemed like a bad dream. I felt so helpless. Sometimes I would look into Noa's wise eyes and feel reassured that everything was going to be all right. But there were other times when I'd lie awake at night in fear. On my worst nights I would just crawl into bed with her, listening to her peaceful breaths, and cry.

I wanted desperately to pray, but I was paralyzed, like when you try to scream in your sleep but no sound comes out. There I was, a rabbi who was supposed to be writing a book of prayers, but my spiritual life was in a state of utter turmoil. As a colleague of mine remarked, "At least God has a sense of humor." Questions and answers would run through my mind: Should I ask God to make this all go away? Well that's not very realistic, is it? Should I ask God to heal her? Healing is for the sick. We really didn't know if Noa was sick or just facing greater challenges than most kids. Should I be angry with God? God didn't do this to her. Nature did. Should I be grateful that my child's condition isn't any worse? Definitely. But I still wished things were better. Should I start writing my book of prayers? I just . . . couldn't.

I couldn't write or work or pray. But I could mommy. In a strange way my spiritual and professional paralysis helped me to be a better mother to my children. I had nothing pulling me away from them. No outside concerns or commitments. My sense of time began to shift. I no longer watched the clock or rushed them because of some schedule I needed to keep. I even stopped carrying a calendar. I turned down requests for teaching and lecturing and stopped attending seminars, meetings, and conventions. I was officially out of the loop. To my colleagues I was one of those promising rabbis who gave it all up to be a mom. But something sacred was beginning to unfold inside me.

When you have a typical child, the early milestones of childhood are marked with excitement and picture taking, but soon you begin to take the progress for granted. You assume that once your child walks, he or she will eventually begin to skip and run and jump. But when you have a child with physical limitations, even the slightest improvement takes on enormous proportions. When your child has received a tricycle from her grandmother as a birthday present, and you have been trying to teach her how to push the pedals for an entire year, and you're wondering whether you shouldn't just give the trike away to someone who might get some use out of it, then suddenly one day without warning there is a slight push and then another, you find yourself with a prayer on your lips: "Thank You, God. May her strength continue to increase before us each day."

My daughter's struggle taught me how to pray again. She taught me to see the unnoticed miracles, the daily blessings. And I am so grateful. Grateful for each morning, for every improvement, for the gift of life. Of course I am still worried. And sometimes I am mournful for all the effort it takes Noa to achieve skills that come as simple reflexes to other children. Sometimes I'm angry. Why should any child face such struggle? Sometimes I'm impatient. I long for dramatic improvement even though I know my child will blossom in her own way and in her own time. But through it all I keep talking to God.

TO PRAY AGAIN

There are many reasons why people who believe in God stop praying. For some it is an event, a crisis or a tragedy, that leaves them feeling hurt, abandoned, and angry at God. A woman in her sixties once came to see me. She had a round, kind face lined with wrinkles. She gestured while she spoke and the soft flesh beneath her upper arms jiggled. She looked as if she ought to be someone's grandmother, but she was no one's grandmother. She was no longer someone's mother. A child who loses his parents is called an orphan. But there is no word in the English language for a mother who has lost her child. The woman told me that ever since her son died at the age of thirty she could no longer pray. Her eyes were wet with tears as she said, "I've quit on God."

What good is prayer if you pray with all your heart and soul and your loved one still dies? Isn't God supposed to help us? Why did God let this happen? Is God even listening? I wish our prayers could instantly alter the course of a fatal disease. I wish we could pray and alleviate all suffering. I wish God had created a world that was free of pain. But that is not the world we have been given. God doesn't always prevent horrible things from happening.

It's natural to be angry at God when tragedy befalls us. Sometimes people come to me with their anger and assume that I will proceed to defend God's ways to them. But I don't. I can't. I too get angry and frustrated and confused.

I grew up believing that God was some kind of superhero who intervenes in our lives to protect the innocent and punish the evil. But there is a problem with this conception of God. Every day the news headlines remind us of the innocent lives that are taken, of the children who go hungry, of the millions of suffering souls. I believe that God is just as outraged as we are by life's unfairness, and just as pained. God is not distant and unfeeling, but compassionate. God suffers when we suffer.

Many people bargain with God when they desperately want something to happen: "God, if You do this for me, I'll do that for You." Then if things don't go their way, they abandon prayer altogether because they assume that God wasn't listening. But I believe God *is* listening. And I believe God answers us. God's answer to our prayers may be very different from the answer we were searching for. God's reply might come as the strength to fight on. It may come as the courage to face what we have been fearing. God's answer may be the ability to accept what we have been denying. Or it may appear as hope in the face of despair. God is neither distant nor deaf. We are not alone. God is present in our lives. When we stop bargaining with God and start opening up our souls to God, our prayers suddenly start working. We can pray for strength and receive strength. Prayer is ultimately an experience, not a request. It is a sense of being connected, of being part of something larger than ourselves. It is an attempt to be in the presence of God.

I no longer look to God to prevent life's ugliness; I look to God to show me the way to prevent the cruelty I have the power to prevent. I no longer see God as a being who can shield me from all harm, but as a presence who has the power to point me toward the holiness that resides in simple acts. Once we stop blaming God for our suffering, we can stop hating God and start listening to God.

I believe it is God who enables us to return to life after tragedy—not by eradicating all suffering but by giving us the strength and the courage to heal what we can heal. God gives us the capacity to appreciate the miracles that surround us each day, the conscience to choose good over evil, the compassion to extend our hands to those who are suffering.

Not all people stop praying because of a single traumatic misfortune. For others, the road away from prayer is a gradual sense of disenchantment. Organized religion failed them in some way. Perhaps there was too much pomp and not enough substance, too much rote learning and not enough meaning, too much formal prayer and not enough inspiration. Or there was too much focus on guilt and not enough focus on love. Perhaps there was too much talk about fund-raising and not enough talk about faith. It's possible they felt neglected in a house of worship. Perhaps they were taught about a God of judgment when they were searching for a God of comfort.

But the fault does not lie in organized religion alone. Many people distance themselves from their faith as a means of rebelling against the traditions of their parents or their society. They dismiss their religion as obsolete without ever taking the time to explore its rich and ancient wisdom. Some distance themselves from God out of a sense of shame and a desire to be accepted into a secular society. There are those who walk away from religious life because it is simply inconvenient, the demands of adherence to faith are too great. They want easy answers, but a life with God is fraught with complexity and mystery. Faith requires things of us that we are not accustomed to giving in our daily lives. A relationship with God implies sacrifice and commitment and patience. Those who expect faith to be effortless, who wish to know God without ever having to reach out with all their hearts and souls, will inevitably be disappointed.

But just as there are forces that lead us away from God, there are forces that lead us back. For some, it is a gradual yearning, a longing for connection, a desire to know God. After years of running away from faith, many people have come to experience the emptiness of a life without God and a community of God. They feel alone, misunderstood, disconnected from their lives in some essential way. They thought prosperity would bring them happiness, but it hasn't. It's brought creature comforts but not a deeper, soulful comfort. They are uneasy about the direction of their lives; they long for meaning. And so they take the first steps on that road back to God. They stumble, they feel inarticulate and awkward; but they walk just the same, with God by their side all the while. And as they make their way back to faith, they are discovering that much has changed during their absence. Religious leaders are breathing new life into faith traditions that have grown heavy and cumbersome with years. Together with their congregations they are seeking to bring God back to earth, to spread the conviction that God lives not just on the pulpit but in our very souls. God's presence fills the universe, animates every living thing, and is as close to us as our own breath. They are teaching people to see that God's relationship with us did not end in scripture, that God is not just the God of history but the God of today and tomorrow and eternity.

They are helping people to perceive God not just as a mighty distant father but as a close and compassionate mother.

For others, a return to God is a response to a specific event, either tragic or joyous. It is true that tragedy can lead us away from God when we assume that God has let us down. But tragedy can also lead us toward God. We seek comfort and meaning in the face of a senseless occurrence. We search for God's stabilizing presence when we feel shaken. Through prayer we can find the stamina to endure a difficult time and the strength to triumph against overwhelming odds.

Joyous moments are the greatest sources of religious inspiration. When we receive a blessing that touches our souls we long to give thanks to God, Source of all blessings. An ancient rabbinic text tells us that in the time to come, when the world is perfected and filled with everlasting peace, all prayers will cease, but thanksgiving prayers will never cease. There will no longer be a need for petitionary prayers because all our hearts' desires will be met. But there will be a never-ending need for prayers of thanks.

There are many reasons for elation—love, marriage, the birth of a child, realizing a dream. But, of course, every single unspectacular day is filled with countless causes for giving thanks. When we take the time to stop and consider all the ways we are blessed each day, we may suddenly become acutely aware of God's presence in our lives. Every breath we take is a cause for celebration. The sky above us, the precious person beside us, the soul within us. Prayer can help us open our eyes and see the wonders we frequently ignore.

Prayer is not a passive activity. Prayer alters us. It awakens us. Our eyes begin to notice beauty where we used to see nothing. Our hearts begin to feel compassion where we used to feel nothing. Our priorities shift. As we talk to God, we receive the encouragement to live up to the potential inside us. Soon we start to see beyond ourselves into the world that is waiting for our help.

PRAYER IS A PRELUDE TO ACTION

Prayer is a way to reach out to God, to share our deepest yearnings, secret wishes, even our unspeakable sins. Prayer not only connects us to God, it also forces us to become intimately acquainted with our own souls. Most of all, prayer helps us to remember our hopes—for ourselves, for our loved ones, for this world—and gives us the strength and courage to realize whatever we most desperately long to achieve.

But prayer is not an end in itself. It is a beginning. An opening up. A hardened heart beats with renewed passion, a dream is revived, a hope is rekindled, a soul starts to believe, a body soon begins to stir. Prayer ignites us to act. Instead of proceeding in a state of numb acceptance, prayer rouses us out of our indifference, it resurrects our outrage, our anger, our longing, our faith, our strength. There are those who dismiss prayer as a palliative, a substitute for action. But they could not possibly be more mistaken. A prayer that leads nowhere is a prayer in vain. True prayer inspires us to become God's partners in repairing this wondrous, imperfect world.

When I was a teenager, my girlfriends and I were often trying to diet. Our motto was: A moment on the lips is a lifetime on the hips. It meant that an act that took just an instant could remain with you forever. I like to apply this phrase to the process of prayer. A prayer takes just a matter of seconds to utter, but its influence on our lives, on our behavior, on our hearts, on our perceptions, can be permanent. A moment on our lips is a lifetime on our souls. A simple prayer can change us, can lead us on the path to healing ourselves and our world.

So pray. Pray for peace, pray for healing, pray for advances in science, pray for the strength to eradicate poverty and disease, pray for the courage to overcome injustice, pray for resolve, pray for others, pray for yourself. Pray to God with all your heart and soul, then gather your might to meet the challenges that lie ahead.

Throughout this book you will find prayers. Some are my own versions of themes already addressed in traditional prayers. Others cover topics not usually found in the liturgy. Please do not view them as replacements for traditional prayers, but rather as supplements that can help you pray when there are no prayers to be found on a particular subject, or when you need words that are a bit more personal than what the prayer book provides.

Please don't use the prayers to replace your own personal expressions of prayer. Use them only as guides, as preludes to your own unique dialogue with God.

You will find prayers and blessings for a wide variety of life experiences. There are daily prayers, prayers to say on joyous occasions, and prayers to say in difficult times. There are prayers for work and for living up to the best in our souls, for love and marriage, for pregnancy and childbirth, for parents and children. There are prayers for healing during illness and for aging. There are prayers of death and of mourning. And there are prayers for our country and for this world.

Some prayers come from my own life. I have cried them, sung them, whispered them to God. Others I can easily imagine when I sit alone in a house of God.

The sanctuary where I write these words is dark and still. The seats are empty. But the air seems strangely saturated. Prayers come to me like echoes from unseen lips: the tears of a motherless bride on the day of her wedding, the request of an elderly man whose wife and soul mate just passed away, the confession of a wayward husband racked with guilt, the gratitude of an infertile couple blessed with a precious adopted child, the elation of a grandmother with her first grandchild in her arms.

I pray that the words in this book will touch your hearts and souls. And that, when the moment is right, you will find your own way to talk to God. If the urge to reach God rises up inside you, don't hold back. Talk to God. Tell God your pain; express your gratitude, your hope, your deepest longing. And listen for a reply.

May you receive an answer that will bring you joy and peace. May God be with you, may health and strength sustain you, may nothing harm you, may wisdom and kindness enrich you, may blessings surround you now and always. Amen. ✹

PRAYERS, BLESSINGS, AND PRONOUNS

This book contains prayers and blessings. Prayers are addressed to God. We bestow blessings upon other people. When we bless someone, we ask God to grant favor to someone we care about. If you find a blessing in this book that you would like to receive, hand it to a loved one and ask him or her to bless you.

It was difficult to arrive at a format for the use of pronouns in the prayers. At first I wanted to include both sexes in each prayer: "God watch over him/her." But it felt impersonal to me, like filling out an application for a driver's license. Then I thought about repeating each prayer twice, once for men and once for women. But that proved too cumbersome. Eventually, I decided to alternate the pronouns arbitrarily. Some prayers say "he" and others say "she." But in most cases there is nothing specifically masculine or feminine about the prayers. Simply change the pronouns to make them apply to your situation.

ONE

Daily Prayer

Daily prayer is the hardest form of prayer. It's natural to turn to God when things go wrong—when you are in pain or when you are frightened or depressed. It's easy to turn to God in times of joy—at a birth or a wedding, or on a holiday. But making the commitment to open your heart up to God every single day is quite a challenge. There are days when we feel moved, and there are days when we feel nothing. All too often, daily prayer seems like a tedious burden. We want our experiences of prayer to be inspirational, exceptional, but daily prayer is rooted in the unspectacular routine of our lives. Most of us see nothing awe-inspiring about getting out of bed in the morning, or grabbing a bite to eat, or nodding off to sleep at night. But we couldn't be more mistaken.

Sometimes it takes an illness to remind us how wondrous it is to wake up healthy, to be able to get out of bed and eat and work. Suddenly, the mundane routines we had taken for granted seem precious. We find ourselves giving thanks for small miracles that we never even noticed before. The first meal after surgery. The first step on our own. The first breath of fresh air. The first night at home in our own bed. Of course, we shouldn't have to suffer an illness in order to be

grateful for all the ways God blesses us. Daily prayer is a fa
more pleasant way to achieve the same goal. Taking the time
to pray heightens our awareness of God's presence in our
lives. It reminds us that God is constantly calling out to us.

One of my favorite quotes from the Jewish mystical teach-
ings is this: "Every blade of grass has an angel that hovers over
it and whispers, 'Grow, grow.'" God is here. God is watching
over us and hoping for us. God is waiting for us to notice the
beauty in every breath we take, the potential in every encounter, the extraordinary possibilities of every ordinary day.

Once, a young man whose wife died in a car accident
came to speak to me. He had a strong and burly build, but his
eyes were soft and sad. He told me that he couldn't pray now,
when he needed God most, because he felt like a hypocrite.
He had never prayed before, and he didn't think he had the
right to start a relationship with God when he had no history
with God. I said to him, "God is already in a relationship with
you. You don't need to introduce yourself. God already knows
you and already loves you. God suffers with you and is longing to hear your voice."

We are in a relationship with God every day whether we
notice it or not. God is waiting for our response.

Morning

When we wake up in the morning, we remember to prepare our bodies for the day ahead of us. We wash, we dress, we eat. Would you ever think of leaving the house without brushing your teeth? And yet we rarely take the time to prepare our souls for the day ahead of us. It doesn't need to take very long. Just a minute or two each morning. But a simple morning prayer can literally transform the way we think, feel, behave, and work. A morning prayer helps to remind us how blessed we are—even on those days when you sleep through the alarm, when the coffee spills on your lap, when the toast burns, when the kids are whining, when nothing seems to be going right. Even brief prayer can give us the courage to confront a difficult day, and it can give us the insight to recognize a miraculous one.

Before you race out the door take a moment. Take a deep breath in, let a deep breath out, and talk to God. Tell God your hopes for the new day and your worries too. And don't forget to notice something to be thankful for this day.

A Morning Prayer

There are so many things I take for granted. May I not ignore them today.

Just for today, help me, God, to remember that my life is a gift, that my health is a blessing, that this new day is filled with awesome potential, that I have the capacity to bring something wholly new and unique and good into this world.

Just for today, help me, God, to remember to be kind and patient to the people who love me, and to those who work with me too. Teach me to see all the beauty that I so often ignore, and to listen to the silent longing of my own soul.

Just for today, help me, God, to remember You.

Let this be a good day, God, full of joy and love. Amen.

A Prayer for the Body

Thank You, God, for the body You have given me. Most of the time I take my health for granted. I forget how fortunate I am to live without pain or disability, how blessed I am to be able to see and hear and walk and eat. I forget that this body of mine, with all its imperfections, is a gift from You.

When I am critical of my appearance, remind me, God, that I am created in Your holy image. If I become jealous of someone else's appearance, teach me to treasure my unique form.

Help me, God, to care for my body. Teach me to refrain from any action that will bring harm to me. If I fall prey to a self-destructive habit, fill me with the strength to conquer my cravings.

Lead me to use my body wisely, God. Guide my every limb, God, to perform acts of compassion and kindness.

I thank You, God, for creating me as I am. Amen.

Food on Our Table

Last winter I went to see an exhibit of Norman Rockwell paintings that was traveling around the country. One painting made a lasting impression on me. The setting is a bustling diner at lunchtime. The scene is so vivid that you can almost hear the chatter and smell the scents of eggs, burgers, and coffee wafting through the air. On one side of a crowded table a Mennonite mother sits beside her young son. Their heads are bowed in silent prayer. This private moment of devotion creates calm in the midst of the clamor. All eyes in the room are fixed on them. The expression on the bystanders' faces is a combination of curiosity and awe. It moved me.

We have the capacity to change the pace and tone of our lives in an instant. We can gobble down our food without even paying attention to what we are eating, or we can take a moment and stop.

Before you eat, take the time to breathe deeply. Look at the food in front of you. Appreciate it. Remember to thank the person who took the time to prepare this food for you. And thank God for the blessed meal before you.

THANKS TO THE COOK

When my husband was courting me, he used to walk me home from synagogue on Saturdays. One day I invited him in. We sat talking for hours sipping tea, and it never occurred to me to offer him something to eat—I didn't know how to cook. At one point I got up to use the bathroom, and he used the occasion to hunt through my cupboards. He was starving. But all he found was a bag of stale potato chips and two cans of tuna. When I returned from the bathroom, I found him looking around my barren kitchen. He picked up a tuna can and asked, "Do you eat it out of the can like a cat?" "Well, yes," I admitted. That night Rob brought me to his apartment and cooked me a magnificent meal. The rest is history. Although every now and then for nostalgia's sake, he opens up a can of tuna and calls, "Here, kitty, kitty."

A Blessing over Food

Thank You, God, for the food on my table and for the cook who, like You, knows the secrets of creation. Thank You for plants, animals, and water, and for my own life, which You nourish and sustain each day. Please, God, answer the prayers of all those who turn to You in need. May all who are hungry be blessed with food. May I never be indifferent to the cries of those in need of my assistance. May I never take my good fortune for granted. Thank You, God, Creator of all. Amen. ✒

Difficult Days

It was a Monday morning. I knew in advance it was going to be a painful day. A member of my congregation was dying. I had been up all night with my one-month-old daughter, Noa, who was doing her best to turn colic into an art form. My two-year-old son, Adi, was busy taking fistfuls of mud from the ficus tree in our living room and dumping them onto the floor. This was our second day in our new home. I had a sinus infection and an ear infection. A friend of mine volunteered to watch my children so that I could visit Marty.

I drove to the hospital, made my way to Marty's room, and saw him lying there ashen and unconscious. His nurse took me aside and told me that he probably would not make it through the night. I thanked her for her honesty. Marty was only fifty. Six months before I had taken a walk with him on the boardwalk that runs along Venice Beach. I had trouble keeping up with his pace. He exercised daily, ate well, had a perpetual suntan, and was forever making fun of my pale, or, as he put it, green, complexion. "You need to get your face out of the Talmud and into the sun, Rabbi." I stood beside Marty and recited the final confessional. Then I blessed him and bade him farewell.

I took the elevator to the lobby, headed back to the parking garage, got into my car, and started driving in a total daze. My mind was on Marty, not the road. I accidentally drove my car onto a cement island that separated the lanes in the parking lot. Embarrassed and shaken, I tried to drive off the island, but my car wouldn't budge. People behind me were honking and shouting. Finally, two men got out of their cars and pushed my car off the island as I steered.

Before returning home I decided to drive back to our old apartment to check if we had left anything behind in the haste of packing. When I got there, I saw that the door was ajar. The painters were there repainting the whole place. I told them that I was the old tenant; they nodded at me. I suddenly realized that I had returned to say goodbye. I bade farewell to my son's lavender bedroom that we had painted ourselves, and to the little yard where we had kept three chickens. I stepped back inside to take a final look out the living-room window, which had a spectacular view of the ocean, and I noticed something on the floor.

The painters had spread drop cloths all over the place, so at first I thought that I must be mistaken. But when I got closer I recognized it. One of the painters was standing on my *tallis*, my prayer shawl. It was the prayer shawl my dean had presented to me and draped over my shoulders on the day I became a rabbi. I asked the painter to step off the cloth, then I picked it up and walked out the door. It was spattered with paint. I sat down on the front step, draped my *tallis* across my lap, and, in honor of Marty, I turned my face to the sun. The warm light felt good against my wet cheeks.

A Prayer for Bad Days

Be with me, God. I feel so lost. I can't seem to escape the dark cloud that is hanging over me today. Help me, God. Give me strength to combat despair and fear. Show me how to put my pain into perspective. Teach me to have faith in the new day that is coming.

Thank You, God, for today's blessings, for tomorrow's hope, and for Your abiding love. Amen.

A Prayer for Those Days When Life Spins Out of Control

When I panic, God, teach me patience.
When I fear, teach me faith.
When I doubt myself, teach me confidence.
When I despair, teach me hope.
When I lose perspective, show me the way—
back to love, back to life, back to You. Amen.

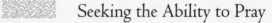 Seeking the Ability to Pray

Having the desire to pray doesn't necessarily lead to prayer. There are numerous obstacles that prevent us from speaking to God. Distractions from outside combine with resistance from inside, and it is no wonder that prayer rarely comes easily. What helps? Make time for daily reflection. Don't feel inhibited by your lack of eloquence. If no great thought enters your heart, just remember to give thanks for something each day. Don't allow guilt or shame to cause you to hide from God. Search for sources of inspiration—the beauty of nature, the love of your family, your health, your hopes for this world. If no words rise up from you, say a prayer for the ability to pray.

A Prayer for the Ability to Pray

Dear God, as I pray, day after unpredictable day,
May the voice of my soul spring forth from my
  lips.
May I turn to You, God, in tears, in laughter, and
  in song.
And may my prayers be answered. Amen. ✒

———

A Prayer for Daily Insight

Open my eyes, God. Help me to perceive what
I have ignored, to uncover what I have for-
saken, to find what I have been searching for.
Remind me that I don't have to journey far to discover something new, for miracles surround me,
blessings and holiness abound. And You are near.
Amen. ✒

Mentors in Unlikely Places

A couple of years ago when we were doing some construction on our home, my husband and I and our two children moved in with his parents. My mother-in-law had just bought a beautiful downy white couch. As you can imagine, they weren't eager for my children to jump on this highly stainable piece of new furniture, and I did my best to keep the kids out of the living room.

The inevitable occurred when my in-laws were gone for the weekend. My son, in search of a napkin, found the nice white couch and proceeded to wipe his hands full of peanut butter and jelly on it. The minute I saw the golden streak across the sofa cushion I started to panic. I called friend after friend asking for advice on how to remove the stain. Soda water was the most common response. Some recommended Shout. Luckily it was a slipcover, and my friend Jane recommended a very reputable dry cleaner. Needless to say, the next morning I arrived at the dry cleaner's at six and waited for him to open the store. He welcomed me in, and I proceeded to tell him the tale of the brand-new white couch with the peanut butter smeared on it and how my in-laws were returning the following day and how I needed his help. The man held the slipcover in his hands, examined it, and said, "It's my experience that the best way to handle a situation like this is honesty. After all, what if I clean the cover and it comes out a different shade of white from the rest of the couch? That would make things much worse. I think you should calmly sit down with your mother-in-law and just explain what happened." When he handed me back the slipcover, I looked at him and said, "You're not a dry cleaner, you're a rabbi!"

The cleaner could have just taken my money and done his best with the slipcover. He could have refused to clean it without offering any advice at all. But he chose to offer me his counsel. He reminded me that being honest was the best path to take. He calmed my fears.

When my in-laws returned the next day, we showed them the stain and explained what had happened, and they didn't seem to mind at all. Or at least they weren't surprised.

A Prayer for the Humility to Learn from Others

You have filled this world with so many good and wise people. Grant me the humility, God, to seek out many teachers. Give me the courage to ask for help, the ability to distinguish wisdom from folly, the willingness to embrace new thoughts.

May my learning lead me to insight, to reverence, to love, and to You. Amen.

Night

We all know how to get our bodies ready for bed. We undress, put on pajamas, brush our teeth. But what about our souls? What do we do with our fears? Our longings? Our hurts? Our inspiration?

A prayer at night can help us embrace sleep instead of fighting it. It can help us to learn from darkness instead of fearing it. It can bring comfort to our minds and hearts. It can transform our worries into awe, our tension into trust, our restlessness into peace.

When you lie down in bed, spend a minute telling God what you need to say. May sweet sleep surround you all night long.

A Night Prayer

With the darkness comes Your light. Earth and sky blend into one, the heavens seem closer now, the day's burdens farther somehow. Your presence is almost palpable.

Watch over me, God, body and soul. Stay beside me through the night. Protect me from harm. Banish my fears. Send me dreams that are sweet, fill my heart with Your peace, set my mind at ease. And, at first light, please, restore me to new life. Amen. ✍

Children at Night

Darkness is frightening. And yet each night we ask our children to face this time of fear alone in their beds. We sing to them and read to them and we kiss them goodnight and then we close the door behind us. Certain objects offer comfort. A favorite stuffed animal, a treasured blanket, a night-light. But a prayer can offer a deeper security. A prayer can leave our children feeling wrapped in love all through the night. A prayer can teach them that they are never alone; that even in sleep, even in darkness, God will watch over them and protect them.

I wrote the following prayer for my children. I say it to them after they recite the traditional Jewish bedtime prayer, the Shema. They say it helps them to fall asleep, especially on those nights when they are feeling particularly frightened of the dark.

A Night Prayer for a Parent to Say to a Child

When you lie down in bed,
    may sweet thoughts fill your head.
When I turn down the light,
may your sleep fill the night.
If the dark makes you fear,
remember I am here,
and God is near,
so sleep, my dear,
sleep, my dear,
sleep.
Amen.

TWO

Prayers for Love and Marriage

You can't rush love.

When I was a congregational rabbi, a man once came to see me because he wanted to know if I could recommend some women in the congregation for him to date. He said that he went on blind dates almost every week. On these dates he would fire off a series of questions: What are your hobbies? What's your favorite pastime? Do you smoke? Do you ski? He claimed that he could tell instantly if the woman was right for him. So far he hadn't exactly struck gold. "I'm looking for new prospects," he said to me. I explained to him that you can't speed through a relationship. You actually have to get to know a woman. You have to break through the period of apprehension. You have to learn what makes her happy and be willing to let down your guard enough to let another person in. None of that work can be accomplished on a single blind date, I told him. I hoped my words were having an impact on this impatient man. He looked at me and said, "Okay, okay, okay, but can you recommend any women to me?" I did—I gave him the name of a good therapist to see.

Love comes in its own time. There is a rush of emotions, a sharing of body and soul. When passion is new and desire is strong, love may feel like a mighty force. But in truth a relationship of love is a fragile entity. Love can flourish only where there is honesty and loyalty, kindness and compromise and trust.

Marriage represents a couple's faith that the love they share is an enduring love. Two individuals make a sacred covenant to create a life together, a home, a family, a future. This leap of faith can lead to untold joy, to deep commitment, devotion, a closeness like no other. But marriage requires constant vigilance and effort. Individuals who enter a marriage thinking it will be easy often become quickly disillusioned when they realize the enormous amount of work it takes to make this sacred bond last. Talking to God can help us find and sustain the rare gifts of love and marriage.

Shrinking and Growing

In the Jewish mystical tradition God created the world through a process called *tzimtzum,* or shrinking. At first God's presence filled the universe, and there was no space for anything else. In order to make room for creation, God chose to contract. Only then could God establish the world and enter into a relationship with it.

If we want to enter into a relationship with any person, we have to be willing to make room for them in our hearts and in our lives.

If you want to live alone, you can decide where all the furniture goes, you can spread your belongings all over the house, you can take up as much space as you want. But if you want to create a life with someone, you have to be willing to compromise, to welcome his taste or her stuff.

If you want to be alone, you can choose where you want to eat and what you want to eat and what movie you want to see after you eat. But if you want to be in a relationship, you have to shrink and make room for someone else's desires.

Only by contracting our needs and wants can we receive the blessings that another person can add to our lives.

A Prayer to Find Love

Open my heart, God; teach me to remove all obstacles I place in the way of love.

Open my mind, God; prevent me from rejecting any person on the basis of superficial flaws.

Open my mouth, God; let my words reflect the beauty and wisdom of my soul.

Open my ears, God; let me be still so that I can truly hear what others are trying to say.

Open my arms, God; give me the strength to be vulnerable, the courage to let down my defenses.

Open my eyes, God; help me find the one I have been praying for.

Please send me my soul mate, God. Amen.

A Prayer of Thanks When Love Arrives

I'm in love. She has entered my heart, my home, my body, my soul. She has entered my life, my days, my every thought and breath. I am full. I never imagined this would happen to me. I had stopped believing.

Thank You, God, for answering my prayer, for restoring my hope, for saving my faith, for creating two people who fit together so perfectly. Amen.

Sexuality

Love arises from the soul. But love is expressed in the body. All humans crave physical affection. Parents cannot love their child in their hearts and remain physically remote. Infants will not thrive properly if they are raised without the comfort of a human touch. A steady diet of caresses can literally save a life.

Romantic love is infused with desire. Sex is the fulfillment of that desire. But sex requires a leap of faith, a hope that the ideal love of the heart will find its counterpart in the flesh. Sex is a holy undertaking, a blessing from heaven. Two bodies and souls intertwine in love and become one. Making love is more than a physical act. It requires profound attention, an offering of the heart. There is no shortcut to intimacy.

Sexuality is a blessing. When two lovers unite in passion, their lovemaking is a sacred act. Their longing is more than a physical hunger, it is a yearning for oneness. It is a desire to concretize ineffable emotions of the soul in the flesh. The Bible refers to sex as "knowing." "And Adam knew Eve . . ." Isn't this the prayer of every person? To be unlocked, freed from the curse of separateness. To be known thoroughly, to be understood. A knowledge that transcends words, that transcends even flesh. This kind of knowing can occur only when two people are prepared to let down the defenses that keep us safe. But the defenses that keep us safe also keep us apart. We have to be willing to open ourselves up. And it's frightening. Without our emotional armor we can get hurt. If we reveal ourselves completely, we will reveal our imperfections. And that requires a great deal of courage and faith. You have to believe that your partner will embrace you with all your faults. And you have to learn to embrace your partner with all his or her faults as well. But unless we are willing to share our bodies and our hearts with another, we can never hope to achieve the magical closeness we have been praying for.

The choice is ours. We can reduce sex to a simple bodily function, or we can exalt sex and encounter our beloved in reverence, gratitude, and awe.

A Couple's Prayer for Holy Sex

Teach us reverence, God, for the sacred joining of our bodies and souls. Remind us to be present in every touch, to be attentive to every response. Prevent us from acting without feeling. Remind us, God, to open our hearts and to shut out all distractions.

Grace us with Your light, God. Let our lovemaking lead us to joy, blessings, and peace. Amen. ✍

A Prayer for Rekindling Passion

The fire is barely flickering, God. Our encounters used to be effortless, we had an instant chemistry. But now monotony and stress have found their way into our bed. And I am frightened, God. I don't want our love to die.

Help us, God, to recapture the passion that once burned so brightly. Remind us of the deep love we share. Prevent us from taking each other for granted. Teach us how to leave the pressures of the day behind.

Guide us, God, to open our hearts and to shut out all distractions. Show us how to transform our predictable routine into a magical encounter of intensity and wonder.

Teach us patience, God, and reverence, for the sacred joining of our bodies and souls. Remind us to be present in every touch, to be attentive to every response. Prevent us from acting without feeling. Grace us, God, with Your light.

Please resurrect our sex life, God, reawaken our desire. Lead us to romance, to rapture, to the blessing of oneness. Amen.

A Painful Breakup

Unfortunately, love isn't always forever. Relationships die, and we must mourn them. Sometimes one person ends a relationship when the other person is still desperately in love. The pain of rejection is difficult to endure. But we have to have faith that our agony will pass, that time will ease our pain, that new opportunities will soon reveal themselves. In time we will learn that we are stronger than we ever imagined. We will find love again.

A Prayer After a Painful Breakup

I miss him so much, God. I can't stop thinking about him. I wish I could just get over it. But it's not that simple. I love him. I don't want to live without him. Help me, God. Heal my pain. Mend my shattered heart. Teach me that I am strong. Remind me that I will love again.

Hear my prayer, God. Let me know You are near. Amen.

Marriage Preparations

A marriage is a covenant and it is also a prayer, a hope that the love two people share is strong enough to last a lifetime. I have joined many couples together in marriage. And I see how much preparation marriage demands. In most cases I have noticed that couples spend more time worrying about the details of a party that will last only a matter of hours than they do preparing for a covenant that will, with hope, last for the rest of their lives. Fretting over the particulars of the party often leads to friction between the bride and groom and between their families. It doesn't take very long before the bickering begins. She wants him to wear a tuxedo; he wants to wear a suit. He wants a certain friend to walk down the aisle; she can't stand the friend. In our final meeting before the wedding, I ask couples to take some time together to write a prayer asking God to bless them on their wedding day and on all the days to follow. The process of writing this prayer usually helps couples to remember what is important and what is insignificant.

A Prayer Before Marriage

I am excited beyond belief, God. And nervous too. I don't take this step lightly. It's an enormous commitment. What a miracle it is to be able to spend the rest of my life with the one I love.

Watch over us, God. Quiet our fears. Be with us on our wedding day and on all the days to follow. Protect us, God, from all harm.

Fill our home with Your light. Fill our hearts with Your love. Remind us never to take each other for granted. Guide us, God, to create a life together filled with respect, loyalty, kindness, and laughter.

Bless us, God, with health and happiness and love. Amen.

Uniting in Marriage

The great rabbi Israel Baal Shem Tov once said that from every human being there rises a light that reaches straight to heaven. And when two souls that are destined to be together find each other, their streams of light flow together in a single, even brighter light that illuminates the heavens.

The marriage ceremony is the moment when two separate people unite to create one family, one future, one light.

A Blessing for Parents to Say When Their Child Marries

May your love for each other grow deeper
with each passing year,
May the bonds between you grow stronger,
May God bless you with children who will bring
you joy, as you have brought joy to us.
May your home be filled with peace and light,
May God shield you from all harm,
May all your prayers be answered.
Amen. ✳

A Blessing for One's Beloved

I love the light in your eyes, the smell of your hair, the sound of your voice. I love the goodness in your heart and the kindness of your deeds. I love our conversations, our home, the family we have created together. I love you. You are a blessing from God.

   May God bless you as you have blessed me with joy and light and love. Amen. ✒

Anniversary

An anniversary is a holy occasion. It marks the day when two separate individuals made a covenant, before human beings and before God, to become one. Sharing presents is certainly a wonderful thing to do. But it should never be the main way we mark this sacred occasion. Offering a gift is a poor substitute for offering up your heart and soul.

Carve out some time on this day for you and your spouse to be completely alone. Open up your heart. Express your love. Allow yourself to receive your spouse's love. Rededicate your lives to each other. Thank God for the gift of love. Ask God to help you rekindle your conversations, your passion, your bond.

An Anniversary Prayer

Marriage is a fragile thing.
Help us, God, to treat it with reverence day after day, year after year.

When we disagree, teach us to do so with compassion.

When we hurt each other, teach us to ask for forgiveness.

When we are tempted by desire, teach us loyalty.

When the stresses of life overwhelm us, teach us to willingly share responsibilities.

When our romance fades, show us the way to passion.

When we fall into a rut, remind us how truly blessed we are.

Thank You, God, for the love we share and for the life we have created together.

Bless us, God, with joy, with love, and with length of years, beneath your sheltering presence. Amen.

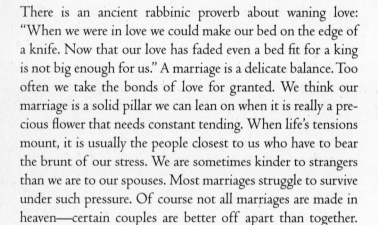

Marital Troubles

There is an ancient rabbinic proverb about waning love: "When we were in love we could make our bed on the edge of a knife. Now that our love has faded even a bed fit for a king is not big enough for us." A marriage is a delicate balance. Too often we take the bonds of love for granted. We think our marriage is a solid pillar we can lean on when it is really a precious flower that needs constant tending. When life's tensions mount, it is usually the people closest to us who have to bear the brunt of our stress. We are sometimes kinder to strangers than we are to our spouses. Most marriages struggle to survive under such pressure. Of course not all marriages are made in heaven—certain couples are better off apart than together. But many marriages suffer from nothing more than weariness and neglect. The power to resurrect a relationship lies in our own hands.

Repairing a marriage is no simple task. Many couples have spent years denying or ignoring problems, and now they must begin the painful process of facing those very same problems. When a marriage is in trouble and the husband and wife fail to confront the aspects of their interaction that need fixing, their relationship will continue to disintegrate. Without honesty, without soul-searching, there is no hope for change and growth. It may be painful and it may take time, but we can revive relationships that have grown weary or cold, we can rekindle romance, mend hurts, change behaviors, we can grow, we can ask for forgiveness, we can forgive. We can and should reach out for help from our community, from a marriage counselor, from our clergy, from our God.

Once, an older man came up to me and announced that he knew the secret to marital bliss. "Tell me what it is," I said. With great pride he replied, "It's simple. I've been married four times." He waited a beat to catch the expression of surprise on my face and then he added, "To the same woman." He explained that the first marriage was when he and his wife were young and carefree. The second was when they were raising their children. The third was when their children grew up and left home. The fourth was when they retired.

I suddenly began to comprehend the wisdom of this man's remarks. Too often couples become frustrated or disappointed because they make incorrect assumptions. Each phase of a marriage requires its own ground rules. You can't expect the dynamics of the carefree relationship to apply when you are raising children. You have to think of it as a new marriage with new expectations, new responsibilities, new stresses, new joys. The same is true for every stage of life. We have to approach marriage as a living organism that needs room to grow and bend and mature. We have to agree to marry the same person over and over again.

A Prayer for a Marriage in Trouble

It was all so easy at first. We went on instinct, fueled by passion and romance and the excitement of something new. But love has a shelf life, God. Milk goes sour, fruit spoils, and our marriage has grown cold.

It never occurred to me, God, that I could be married and alone, married and numb, married and celibate.

Help us, God. Show us the way to reclaim all that we once shared. Raise us up out of this rut; save us from pride, from resentment, from temptation. Save us from cruelty, jealousy, and anger.

Awaken our desire, God, remove the hurt from our hearts, the boredom from our eyes. Breathe new life into our days, our conversation, our touch, our bed.

Give us strength, God, perseverance, resilience, the stamina to fight for our marriage. Bless our efforts, God. Fill our home with Your light; furnish it with warmth, laughter, and peace.

Show us the way, God. Lead us on the road back to intimacy, back to meaning, back to hope, back to joy, back to each other. Amen.

 Fighting Temptation

When my book *To Begin Again* was published, I wasn't prepared for the numbers of people who began phoning me at home. I soon realized that I needed a separate work line. I was leafing through a newspaper when I saw an add for a voice mail company. For just a few dollars a month I could rent a phone number that people could leave messages on. This was perfect. I called the company, set up my voice mail message, and congratulated myself for the brilliant idea. I could relax in peace now and respond to the messages whenever it was convenient. But there was no peace in store for me.

Each time I checked my messages, there would be a few calls for speaking engagements and many more calls from men who seemed to be unusually interested in meeting me. I thought the picture on my book jacket came out quite nice, but now it seemed it had become a source of attraction. A typical mild message went something like this: "I saw your picture and I like the way you look. Call Steve." The more graphic messages I simply can't repeat. Something very strange was happening, and I decided that it couldn't possibly be due to my book jacket photo. These men did not sound like they had found me as they were browsing in the inspiration section at Barnes & Noble.

I returned the calls for the speaking engagements, but I didn't even begin to know what to do with the scores of male suitors. I could have requested a new voice mail number, but there were too many legitimate people who had been given that number, and I didn't want to lose touch with them. Then one day I got a clue. In a message a man said, "Hi, Island Girl. I saw your picture on Desert Island. Call Bill." Island Girl? And what in the world was Desert Island? I spent all day trying to figure it out. I called information and checked the Yellow Pages, but no luck. It was late at night when my husband had the brainstorm: Maybe it was an Internet address. We sat down at the computer and typed desertisland.com—and, behold, it was a pornography site. It was the United Nations of naked women. But still I couldn't figure out what this all had to do with me. Then I found her. She was Asian and topless with large breasts and a grass skirt that could have used a lot more grass. And below her photo was *my* voice mail number. My husband and I both fell on the floor in laughter. When I recovered, I sent off an e-mail to the home page address, explained the mishap, and asked them to update Island Girl's phone number immediately.

Days passed but my male callers weren't letting up. And I never received a reply to my e-mail. So I got back onto the website to look for a new solution. I found a second picture of Island Girl and this time there were two numbers listed. The first one was mine. I decided to call the second number. The phone rang a few times and then a woman with an Asian accent picked up. I said, "Is this Island Girl?" She said, "Yes, honey. I like girls too." "No, you don't understand," I quickly explained. "There's a mistake. You have my phone number listed under your picture. You need to change it. You're losing a lot of business because I'm getting your calls." She asked, "Are you getting a lot of work? I hardly get *any.*" I said, "No, you don't understand, I'm not in your line of work. I'm a rabbi. I just want you to change the number under your picture." She didn't seem to know what a rabbi was, but she said she would correct the problem. And we hung up.

Within a matter of days the lust-filled messages disappeared, and I breathed a sigh of relief. Now I could concentrate on all the real messages and return them in order. One was a very polite message from a man named Jeff (I've changed the name) who worked at a movie studio. I called Jeff back, and he picked up the phone. I said, "Hi. This is Rabbi Naomi Levy returning your call." He said, "Who?" I repeated myself, but he still seemed confused. I said, "I have a message on my voice mail from you." And then it hit me. I asked him, "Did you get the number from the Desert Island website?" And Jeff said, "Can you hold on, please?"

He went to close his office door, then got back on the phone. "Is this some kind of joke? Are you really a rabbi?" "Yes," I replied, "But there was a mix-up and the pornography site accidentally listed my number." I felt bad for Jeff. The poor schlemiel called a prostitute, and he got a rabbi.

Suddenly Jeff started to spill his soul to me. He was married, he loved his wife. But after his son was born, their sex life had fallen apart. Jeff had been keeping Island Girl's number in his desk for weeks before he got up the nerve to call. He said he had never called a prostitute before, that he was just looking for some sexual release. I told Jeff that searching outside his marriage for fulfillment wasn't going to solve his problems. It would only add to them. He needed to start looking inside his marriage if he truly wanted things to improve. I explained that it is common for couples to experience a disruption in their sex life when a child is born, that it didn't mean his wife had stopped loving him. He seemed relieved. Then we talked about temptation and about ways to fight it. When we were finished speaking, Jeff thanked me and said he thought God had a good sense of humor.

God certainly did find an original way to keep Jeff from straying.

A Prayer to Fight Temptation

I never imagined this could happen to me, God. I love my wife. And yet here I am thoroughly overwhelmed by longing for another woman. My heart is pounding, my body aches for her, my thoughts keep returning to her even though I try with all my might to shut them out.

Help me, God. I don't want to do something I know I will regret. But something inside me doesn't seem to care about that right now. Something inside me wants to be with her at any cost. It's a dangerous side of me. A reckless, selfish side of me that doesn't care about consequences. I know there will be consequences, God.

Please give me strength, God. When temptation rises within me, help me to conquer it. When my yearning cries out, teach me to withstand it. When I feel helpless to fight my desire, remind me that I possess the power to master my urges.

When I am lost and in need of direction, show me the way, God, back to my marriage, back to my life, back to love. Amen. ✒

Unfaithfulness

A breach of trust does not have to lead to the collapse of a marriage. When a partner has been unfaithful, it is natural for couples to panic and believe there is no hope for their relationship. People make grave mistakes that are hurtful to those they love. But repair is possible if someone is committed to healing the damage he or she has caused. Seeking the counsel of a professional who can provide wisdom and guidance can be invaluable. Of course, restoring trust is no easy task. You must be sincere in your apology, take full responsibility for your actions, and rededicate yourself to a life of loyalty, honesty, and devotion.

A Prayer for Guidance When One Has Been Unfaithful

What have I done, God? What was I thinking? I wasn't thinking at all. I was wild, reckless, frantic. But now my mind has awakened, and my thoughts have come flooding in. The guilt. It is as relentless as the passion that hounded me just days ago. It pursues me and won't let me be. There's no way to erase what I have done. I have lied and cheated and deceived. I have betrayed the one person I love more than any other. I have violated a holy covenant. It takes so much energy just to look him in the eyes. I can't bear to look into his eyes. Is there hope for repair, God? Is there room for forgiveness? The compulsion to confess is overwhelming. It takes enormous restraint to say nothing. Should I tell him, God? Or should I keep it to myself? Help me, God. I don't want to lose him. I don't know what to do. I'm ashamed to be asking for Your direction now, God, when I know I should have turned to You before I strayed. If only I had talked to You, perhaps I would not be in this awful mess right now. Please forgive me, God. Forgive me for hiding from You, for deceiving my husband, for allowing my lust to overpower my love. Show me Your love, God. Please don't hide from me. Please, God, help me, I don't want to lose it all. Teach me, God, how to change. Fill me with the strength to resist temptation. Show me the way back to integrity, back to faithfulness, back to my life, back to my love. Amen.

Divorce

Not all marriages are made in heaven. Some couples are mismatched. A choice that seemed right initially turns out to be wrong. People outgrow each other; their love withers. Some marriages are fraught with cruelty and conflict. Some are passionless and cold. Some people view divorce as a sin. But I believe there are times when the best decision a couple can make is the decision to part.

Divorce is the death of a marriage. It is painful. Anyone who assumes divorce will lead to instant happiness is horribly mistaken. As with any death, mourning is a gradual process. Healing takes time.

Every person approaches divorce differently. Some look upon divorce as an act of self-preservation. For others it is a source of shame and a symbol of failure. Some couples part with relative ease and mutual respect. Others grow spiteful and vindictive. When a couple has children, divorce is not the end of their relationship. Parents will be forever tied to each other through their children.

The prayers that follow ask God for the strength to heal from divorce and for the wisdom to part in dignity and grace.

A Divorce Prayer

Our marriage is over, God. It really does feel like a death. The death of our dreams, our hopes, our home, our love, our life together.

Help us, God, save us both from vindictiveness and cruelty. Let us not prolong this divorce. Teach us a way to move forward with decency, integrity, and honesty. Show us how to divide our assets fairly, to determine our children's custody and future wisely.

Give us the strength, God, to part with dignity and grace in honor of the life we once shared. Amen.

———

A Prayer for Healing from the Pain of Divorce

I am holding it all together on the outside, God, but inside my heart is crushed. I never imagined the future without him. I never imagined myself without him.

Help me, God. Give me the courage to face the past and to learn from it. Remind me to take the time to grieve for all that is no more. I feel so alone. Be with me, God. Teach me to believe that there is hope for me, that I will find love again.

Heal my heart, God. Fill me with the strength to gather up all the broken pieces, and begin again. Amen.

A Second Marriage

When I think back on all the weddings I have performed, some of my favorite ceremonies have been for second marriages. There is something wondrous about having another chance at love. The bride and groom know how fragile marriage is, I don't really have to remind them. They focus more on the covenant they are making and less on the party they are throwing. They have gained wisdom from the pain they endured. There is an enormous appreciation for the gift of new love, and at the same time there is a knowledge that marriage requires far more than love. For those who have been divorced, a second marriage is an opportunity to get it right, to do things differently. For those whose spouses have died, a second marriage is an affirmation that there can be love and joy and life after death.

Holly and Frank both knew how they wanted to be married this time around. They didn't want to orchestrate a huge celebration, they told me; their greatest celebration would be the moment they could call themselves husband and wife. At the appointed hour their loved ones all showed up in my study. It was cramped, but the intimacy of the moment felt right.

Holly wore a simple spring dress, but there was no mistaking who the bride was. She was aglow. Four friends held up a *tallis*, a prayer shawl, as the wedding canopy. Frank and Holly stood proudly beneath its shelter. There was no band, no emcee, no photographer, no party planner, no florist, no caterer. Before me there was simply a couple deeply in love and surrounded by love. And there was God, whose presence felt very close. It was a beautiful way for two people to begin a life together.

A Prayer for a Second Marriage

There was a time when I feared that I would never love again, God. And here I am about to marry the one I love. I have to keep reminding myself this is not a dream. I am so grateful to You, God, for opening my eyes and my heart to love, for restoring my hope, my faith, and my life.

We pray that you will be with us, God, on our wedding day and on all the days to come. Watch over us, God, bless us, help us to create a life together where our love can thrive and flourish.

Thank You, God, for the gift of a new beginning. Amen. ✍

THREE

Prayers for Pregnancy and Childbirth

Pregnant women tell me this all the time: "If men were the ones having the babies, there would be *plenty* of prayers about pregnancy and childbirth." I think they're right. For centuries, most religious traditions excluded women from full participation in ceremonial life and leadership. It's no wonder, then, that so few prayers are written from a woman's perspective. An entire realm of wisdom, courage, and faith is absent from our liturgy.

Is there a greater miracle than childbirth? Throughout history women suffered, labored, and lost their lives for the sake of bringing forth new life. They chose life in the face of despair, they looked to the future when an uncertain present offered few signs of hope. I can think of no human experience that is more worthy of our blessings, prayers, and praise.

There are no words to describe the mysterious journey from conception to childbirth. So many emotions intermingle: joy, fear, wonder, uncertainty, gratitude, awe, love. God seems very near. As I explained in the Introduction, it was my desire to reach out to God during my pregnancy that led me to begin writing my own prayers. The process transformed my spiritual life. I used to think that prayer came from a book; now I know that it comes from the depths of the soul.

A Prayer for a Couple Hoping to Conceive

Our love is strong. We both want, more than anything, to bring a new life into this world. Bless us with a child, God. Help us, God. Let us conceive, God. Let our love bear fruit. When our bodies and souls unite in love, let the seed of life take root.

Make us fertile, God. Be with us, God; watch over us, hear our prayer. Amen. 🖋

Miracles Do Happen

Not long ago, a woman came up to me with an adorable little girl in her arms. She told me she'd had quite a difficult time conceiving and even more difficulty maintaining a pregnancy. She was tired and dejected and spent many nights in tearful prayer. But after six miscarriages she became pregnant and brought forth the child she was holding. She said to me, "Rabbi Levy, I'd like you to meet my daughter. We named her Miracle."

A Prayer When One Experiences Infertility

We have been praying for a child, God, but month after month our hopes have turned to disappointment. Bless us with a child, God. Help me, God. Let me conceive. Turn my envy into love, my despair into hope, my anxiety into calm, my tears into joy. Bless my doctors with wisdom and skill. Let the seed of life be planted and let it take root. Make me fertile, God. Be with me, God; watch over me, hear my prayer. Amen.

A Prayer When a Woman First Learns She Is Pregnant

Thank You, God, for the sacred life that is growing inside me. It is a miracle. I feel blessed, elated, powerful, proud.

Grace me with an easy, healthy pregnancy, God. Guard me and my unborn child from all harm. May my baby grow in health and strength with each passing day. Help me prepare my body and my heart to receive this precious new life.

Let this be a beautiful healthy child, full of goodness and joy. Thank You, God, Creator of all. Amen. ✔

A Daily Prayer During Pregnancy

Bless me, God.
Let me carry this child in health and ease.
Let no harm or misfortune come to me or to the
precious life growing within me.
Let labor begin in its proper time.
Let me bear my child without too much pain.
Let my child be born in health into a world filled
with peace.
May my child grow to bring goodness and blessing
into this world.
For the miracle of creation that is taking place inside
me, I thank You, God, Creator of all. Amen. ✹

————

A Prayer During a Difficult Pregnancy

Help me, God. Help me to endure this time of
pain and discomfort. Remind me that this
unpleasantness will pass. In the end may my labors
be rewarded with a precious new life.

Fill me with strength, God, with patience and
stamina and faith. Grant me health, God, and grant
health to the sweet, sacred life growing within me.
Amen. ✹

A Prayer for the End of the Ninth Month

God, as the days of my pregnancy draw to a close, I want to thank You for allowing me to carry this precious life inside me, for the gift of watching and feeling my baby grow.

As the hour of labor approaches, I pray to You, God, for the strength and the courage to face and endure labor. May my labor not be too painful or too long. Let my delivery go smoothly. Grant my doctors, nurses, and midwives the wisdom and skill to care for my child and for me properly. But most of all, God, I pray that our baby will be born healthy, swaddled in blessings and in love. Amen.

A Prayer During Labor

Help me, God, to bear these pains. Speed my labor, let me open wider and wider with each contraction. Grant me a swift delivery without complications. Ease my pains, God, calm my fears. Grace my doctors, nurses, and midwives with the skill and wisdom to properly care for my child and for me. I entrust my body and soul, and the body and soul of my precious baby, into Your protecting hands. Watch over us, God. Shelter us, shield us from all harm. Let me soon hear the blessed cries of my child born in health and surrounded in love. Amen.

Breathing in Strength

Randy was enduring an excruciating contraction when I entered her hospital room. She closed her eyes and breathed deeply until the pain subsided. Her husband, Jim, was massaging her back lovingly. Randy had been in labor for some eighteen hours by then, but things were pretty much at a standstill. She wasn't dilating; her labor wasn't productive. She was drenched in sweat and frightened, but her eyes exuded a deep confidence and strength. Randy looked up at me and asked, "Can you say a prayer for me and the baby?" I placed one hand on her head and one on her belly and offered a breathing prayer. I spoke the words; she did the work. I sat with her for about half an hour repeating this chant over and over again. Suddenly a smile appeared across Randy's face. She told me that she felt an opening up. She called the nurse in to check her, and the nurse announced, "You're nine centimeters dilated!"

I won't promise you that this prayer can replace Pitocin, the drug given to induce labor. But who knows, maybe it can give your cervix a little extra encouragement. Have your coach read it to you again and again as you close your eyes, relax, and breathe deeply, in and out, to its rhythm.

A Breathing Prayer
WORDS OF ENCOURAGEMENT AND FAITH
TO SAY TO A WOMAN IN LABOR

(In)   Breathe in strength. A child is coming.

(Out)   Breathe out fear. These pains will pass.

(In)   Breathe in calm. Your child is coming.

(Out)   Breathe out tension. These pains will pass.

(In)   With each contraction. Your child is coming.

(Out)   Let your body relax. Relax.

(In)   Breathe in courage. God is with you.

(Out)   Breathe out exhaustion. You are far stronger
than you know.

(In)   Let your body open. Your child is coming.

(Out)   God will unlock the gate. Open the gate.

(In)   We'll soon call you mother. Your child is coming.

(Out)   You'll hear your baby cry. These pains will pass.

(In)   Breathe in faith. A healthy birth awaits you.

(Out)   Breathe out worry. God will bless you with joy.

Keeping Things in Perspective

I recently had a conversation with a woman who teaches natural childbirth classes. The teacher had just given birth to her own daughter by cesarean section, and instead of being elated she was disappointed. She told me that she felt as if she had failed. She had been thoroughly prepared for a vaginal delivery, she knew all the moves and breaths to take, and she was utterly demoralized by the fact that she had required a C-section.

I have witnessed this response numerous times. Some women feel like failures because they broke down and begged for an epidural. There are women who think they are bad mothers because they did not breast-feed their children.

I told this teacher that she was losing sight of how blessed she was. She was healthy. Her newborn daughter was healthy. She'd had a smooth and swift delivery. I added that her experience with the cesarean section was going to make her a better natural childbirth teacher. She could now speak from experience about when things don't go as planned. As much as we wish to believe we are in control, we must learn the art of surrender. She could now begin to teach couples to embrace the full mystery and the miracle of childbirth.

 Those Who Assist at a Birth

When I was a congregational rabbi, there was a Catholic church right across the street from my synagogue. The priest and I were the same age, we entered our positions at exactly the same time, and we quickly became close friends. Whenever we got together, we would commiserate about the burdens of spiritual leadership. We would encourage, counsel, and comfort each other. We followed different religious traditions, but we shared a deep and passionate faith in the same God.

One night I bumped into him in the lobby of the local hospital. We were both there tending to congregants. He told me he was visiting a dying man. I told him that I had just witnessed the birth of a baby girl. He looked at me and said, "No one has ever asked me to attend a birth. You are so lucky that your congregants welcome your presence at such a sacred time." As a woman rabbi I do have unique access to the miracle of childbirth, and I feel blessed to be called upon to add my prayers at this wondrous time.

The moment of birth is a miracle. People who are present often want to offer up words of gratitude to God. But they don't know what to say. I encourage them to speak to God freely from their hearts and to bless their newborn from the depth of their souls. Physicians and nurses who deliver babies do not always take the time to acknowledge the wonder they are engaged in. To them, birth can become a joyous but mundane routine. I wrote this blessing for my obstetrician. He told me that it helps him acknowledge the sanctity of each birth and the holiness of his profession. This blessing can be said by anyone who takes part in a birth and wants to give thanks.

A Prayer for All Who Assist at a Birth
PHYSICIANS, NURSES, MIDWIVES, BIRTHING COACHES, LOVED ONES

I thank You, God, for granting me the opportunity to participate in the miracle of creation. Blessed are You, God, Creator of all. Amen.

The prayers that follow can be recited at the moment of birth. Many families have been incorporating them into naming ceremonies and welcoming rituals for their children.

A Prayer When the Child Is Born

Welcome, welcome to this breathtaking world. We have been waiting for you. Waiting to see your beautiful face, to hear the sound of your cry, to kiss you, hold you, rock you. You are the fruit of our love, of our hearts, of our souls.

We have prayed for this day, and now it is here. But no amount of anticipation could have prepared us for you. You are a miracle. You are a gift from God. You are ours.

May God watch over you in love and bless you with health. How can we express our gratitude to You, God? You have sent us a perfect blessing.

Thank You, bless You, Source of all life. Amen. 🖎

A Mother's Prayer After Birth

Thank You, God. Thank You for seeing me through this birth. For giving me this blessed child. Help me, God. Help my body heal quickly so that I can tend to my baby. Restore me to strength, God. Bless me with the wisdom to understand each cry, and the skill to soothe it. Infuse me with the mysterious powers of a mother's intuition.

Be my guide, God; stay with me through sleepless nights, send me stamina to sustain me, never leave me. Amen.

A Grandparent's Prayer for a New Grandchild

Gift of God, precious child, miracle, my little one. Lay your head on my shoulder. It seems that it was yesterday that I held your mother in my arms just this way. You are a sweet blessing to me, a tiny messenger of joy. Welcome to this magnificent life.

May God grace you with all things that are good and shield you from all harm. May the bonds of our family be your strength. May our love be your comfort. May our faith sustain you. May God be with you, now and always. Amen.

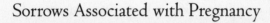 Sorrows Associated with Pregnancy

Life is full of disappointments, challenges, and difficult deci-
sions. But disappointments associated with pregnancy are
particularly painful. The contrast between the longing for
new life and the inability to fulfill that hope is a source of
deep sorrow. Often, friends trying to be helpful may offer
words of comfort that are no comfort at all. They may try to
cheer couples out of sadness instead of allowing them to
experience that sadness. They will say to an infertile couple,
"It's not so bad, you can always adopt," not taking into
account just how devastating infertility can be. They may say
to a woman who has miscarried, or even worse, to a woman
who has suffered a stillbirth, "Don't worry, you can always
have more children." That may be true, but it does not diminish the anguish or mourning of that woman.

Turning to God in these difficult times can be a source of
enormous strength, comfort, and healing. We don't have to
pretend to be all right in front of God. We can expose ourselves, express our grief. God is not scared of our pain. God
shares our pain and God can heal our pain. When we pray to
God for stamina, we may receive the strength to fight on.

A Prayer When One Suffers a Miscarriage

I am crushed, God. Just yesterday I felt so blessed, and now I feel hollow, empty. Why, God? Why did this pregnancy have to end?

I know this miscarriage was not my fault, but I still feel as if I failed somehow. I want to be filled with hope once more, God. I want to be filled with life once more.

Help me, God. Heal me. Let me begin again. Let life take root inside me once more. Remind me that tomorrow is a new day full of promise and possibility.

Lead me, God, on the path back to life, back to hope, back to joy. Amen.

The Termination of a Pregnancy

There aren't many prayers that address the termination of a pregnancy. The decision to end a pregnancy is a painful process that very few women take lightly. A woman who has terminated her pregnancy may feel an overwhelming need to pray. She may long to reach out to God for healing and support—especially if she chose to keep her decision a secret and received no support or comfort from anyone. God is always here to provide compassion and healing, strength and love.

A Prayer After the Termination of a Pregnancy

I made a decision, God, to terminate my pregnancy. This choice was not made lightly. I prayed, I meditated, I searched my soul for an answer. I knew in my heart that I should not complete this pregnancy.

You know my heart, God. You know my pain. You know my anguish. In your infinite wisdom, I pray that You will glean the spark of potential life and plant it where it may grow and flourish.

Help me, God. Shield me from the reproach of those who do not know my heart. Teach me how to overcome feelings of shame and guilt.

Let me begin again, God. Lead me to new hope, to new joy. Hear me, heal me, never leave me. Amen.

Stillbirth

A couple enters the maternity ward with great excitement. They expect to return home with their newborn child. But instead of celebrating life, they must mourn death. There are those who encourage them to sweep this whole nightmare under the rug. But how do you forget such a crushing blow? I have prayed with couples through the grief of stillbirth. And more than anything else, I have been overwhelmed by the depth of their love and the strength of their faith.

A Prayer When One's Child Is Stillborn

I never got to know you.
I felt you inside me. I worried over you. I dreamed about you. I grew with you. I picked a name for you. I was expecting you. I was so looking forward to raising you and watching you grow. But that's not ever going to happen. And I feel very angry and very sad. I wanted to keep you safe, but I couldn't protect you. I couldn't save you from everything that went wrong.

Heal my heart, God, restore my soul. Be with me in my sorrow, surround me with Your comfort. Revive my hope, God; help me to believe that I will come to know blessings and joy once more.

I entrust him to You, God. Take care of him. Watch over him. Protect him. Shelter him with gentleness and love. As I would. Spread Your peace over him.

Hear me, God. Heal me, God. Amen.

A Prayer for Accepting Infertility and Exploring Adoption

God, we want more than anything to have a child. We have tried all the techniques our doctors have to offer. We have lived through a roller-coaster ride of hope and excitement, disappointment and sorrow. I am tired, God. My body is tired.

I still believe in the possibility of a miracle, but perhaps a biological child is not the miracle You have in store for us. I am sad that I may never have the privilege of carrying my child, but perhaps there is a child waiting somewhere at this very moment who is destined to be ours.

We are ready now, God, to begin to explore the opportunity of adoption. Give us the courage, God, to embark on this new journey. Renew our hope. Fill us with the determination and the patience we will need to see this through.

Bless us, God, with a child. Hear this prayer, God. Amen.

FOUR

Prayers for Parents

Becoming a parent is humbling. It is also sacred. You have brought a blessed new life into this world and it is now your task to guard it and to nurture it. And you soon discover that there is a hidden river of love that runs through you straight to your soul. It is a love bound to your very life force. But there is a weakness that comes too. A knowledge that you are small and helpless. It is easier to control an entire legion of soldiers than it is to control one little snotty-nosed kid. And then of course there is the fear. From that fear comes the incessant prayer: Let no harm come to this child. So you preach the parents' catechism: Never talk to strangers. Don't step into the street. Put on your sweater. Don't run with that stick in your hand. Eat your vegetables. Swim close to shore. Inevitably you must ask yourself whether you are the very thing you fear most: the cause of harm to your child. Your shortcomings, your failings, your neuroses, your personality flaws, are all sources of pain and disappointment. Parenthood urges you to strive for better, to reach for more. It inspires you to become more patient, more tolerant, more humble, more loving, more accepting, more honest, more responsible, more generous, and more selfless than you ever imagined.

A Parent's Prayer for Patience

When my child tests me, teach me, God, how to respond with wisdom.

When I grow irritable, send me patience.

When my fury rages, teach me the power of restraint.

When I become fixed in my ways, teach me to be flexible.

When I take myself too seriously, bless me with a sense of humor.

When I am exhausted, fill me with strength.

When I am frightened, fill me with courage.

When I am stubborn, teach me how to bend.

When I act hypocritically, help me to align my deeds with my values.

When mundane pressures threaten to overwhelm me, help me to remember how truly blessed I am.

When I lose my way, God, please guide me on the road back to joy, back to love, back to peace, back to You. Amen. ✒

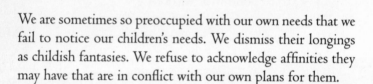

We are sometimes so preoccupied with our own needs that we fail to notice our children's needs. We dismiss their longings as childish fantasies. We refuse to acknowledge affinities they may have that are in conflict with our own plans for them.

I once read an article about Leonard Bernstein's childhood. Apparently his father, Sam, was opposed to young Leonard's interest in music. He thought that pursuing a life in music was a waste of time. He expected his son to work in the family's beauty supply business. This inflexibility obviously led to quite a bit of friction between father and son. Leonard Bernstein persisted in his dream and became one of the greatest composers and conductors of the twentieth century. Eventually, his father acknowledged the mistake he made. Sam said in an interview in *The New Yorker* magazine: "Every genius has a handicap. Beethoven was deaf. Chopin had tuberculosis. Well, someday the books will say, 'Leonard Bernstein had a father.'"

Let us pray that we do not become our children's handicap. Instead, let us nurture our children to realize all the gifts that God has given them.

A Prayer for Bestowing Love Wisely

Love is a great blessing I have to offer.
Help me, God, to give my child a love that
nourishes and heals.
A love that soothes and comforts.
A love that is steady and eternal.
A love that is free from judgment and conditions.
A love that does not seek to smother or control.
A love that respects my child's needs.
A love that instills confidence and independence,
that sets boundaries and limits.
A love that is expressed not by spoiling my child
with tangible gifts, but by offering up things
that can never be measured:
my attention, my affection, my creativity,
my heart.
Thank You, God, for filling me with the capacity
to feel and express this holy emotion.
May I love wisely and generously. Amen. ✿

Offering a Blessing

As the Sabbath begins on Friday night, it is a Jewish tradition for parents to bless their children. I love this tradition. There is no more beautiful way to express your love and your hopes than to place your hands on your child's head and utter a blessing. My children look forward eagerly to receiving their weekly blessing, and when guests come for dinner their children usually turn to their parents and request a blessing as well.

I wrote this blessing for parents to say over their children. But when I shared it with people, they started using it to bless their spouses, their siblings, their parents, their friends. So please feel free to bless anyone you wish. I recommend that you place your hands over the head of the person you are blessing. That way you can offer up not only your words and your heart but also the loving power of your touch.

A Blessing for a Parent to Say to a Child

May all the gifts hidden inside you find their
way into the world,
May all the kindness of your thoughts be
expressed in your deeds,
May all your learning lead to wisdom,
May all your efforts lead to success,
May all the love in your heart be returned to you,
May God bless your body with health and your
soul with joy,
May God watch over you night and day and pro-
tect you from harm,
May all your prayers be answered.
Amen. ✘

Adoption

At one A.M. the sound of sirens echoed along the Brooklyn streets toward the scene of a blaze raging out of control. Fire-fighter John Kroon climbed a ladder and broke through a window of the small apartment. A thick cloud of black smoke filled the air. Elayna Allen, a thirty-year-old woman, was lying unconscious on the floor. He picked her up and passed her outside into the waiting arms of a fellow rescuer. From the intensity of the heat, John feared that the room would soon be in flames. But he wasn't leaving yet. There was a child in this apartment. He was sure of it. He groped along in the darkness, trying to feel around for any sign of life. Nothing. He reached under a bed and pulled something out. A stuffed animal. He reached under again and this time found what he was looking for. A three-year-old girl was huddled in a corner beneath her bed. John held her in his arms and whisked her to safety.

When the ambulance reached the hospital, Elayna Allen was pronounced dead. Her daughter, Francine, was fighting for her life. She remained in the ICU for some time, and then miraculously she started to improve.

In the hospital Francine clung to her nana, her grand-mother Evelyn, the only immediate family she had left. But

Evelyn was an elderly woman who was legally blind and in failing health. She knew she would soon need to find someone to adopt her granddaughter.

Michele Sullum was studying to become a rabbi and doing a hospital chaplaincy internship at NYU Medical Center. One day, Michele was asked to offer a prayer for a little girl. That's how they met. During their first few meetings, Francine would cower and cling to her nana. But soon she began to open up.

Francine was an adorable little girl with enormous blue eyes and wavy brown hair. Whenever Michele came by to visit the children's ward, Francine's face would light up, and she would shout, "My Shell!" That's what Francine called her, as if Michele were her own personal treasure. Michele fell in love with Francine. She couldn't get over the way this small child greeted life with such joy given all that had happened to her.

Evelyn asked Michele if she and her husband, Jacob, might be interested in adopting Francine. Deep in her heart Michele felt that this situation was somehow ordained. When Jacob came to meet Francine, the two of them took to each other immediately.

There were some friends who cautioned Michele and Jacob against making an impetuous decision. They spoke about how difficult it might be to raise a child who had suffered such a severe trauma. They were young and would soon have children of their own. But none of these arguments dissuaded Michele and Jacob.

After much soul-searching, they decided they were ready to adopt Francine. Soon there was an outpouring of support. Friends, family, and even absolute strangers began showering them with children's furniture, toys, and clothing. Michele and Jacob knew that this was a giant step to take. But Francine had entered their lives and their hearts, and there was no way that they were going to let her go.

Today Francine is a happy, healthy nine-year-old girl. She loves her parents desperately, and she knows just how much they love her. She is in close contact with her nana, and she is doted on by all her grandparents. On her dresser there is a framed picture of her mother, Elayna, holding her. Michele once told her daughter, "She's watching you when you sleep." Francine is full of joy, energy, and life. She does have a deep fear of the dark, which probably stems from that awful night when the fire struck. She is very wise for a child of nine. She knows that bad things can happen, that life can be uncertain and unfair. She doesn't take for granted all the good things that have happened to her. She desperately wants to have a little brother or sister. And she is a serious fan of *The Powerpuff Girls.* It's a cartoon about three little girls who save the world from disaster. Francine loves superheroes. Her idols are people who rescue others.

Michele and Jacob would like to give Francine the sibling she has been asking for, but it hasn't been easy for them. Last November, Michele suffered her third miscarriage. She said to me, "Francine is a gift in so many more ways than we realized at that time." Although they are disappointed that they may never be able to have a biological child, Michele and Jacob don't feel the void that many infertile couples experience. They have a child who is the source of deep joy and love. And they are hoping to adopt their second child.

Sometimes we wait and hope for God to answer our prayers. Adoption is one of those situations in which individuals take steps to answer their own prayers. In the process of realizing their prayers, they are given the unique opportunity to answer a child's prayers. And whenever a child's prayer is answered, I believe God smiles and sighs a deep sigh of relief.

A Prayer of Gratitude for an Adopted Child and for All Children

I have carried you
in my dreams, in my heart,
in my every prayer.
Today I hold you in my arms,
beautiful, holy, miracle.
I am full.
Thank You, God,
for this sacred, blessed child.
My child.
Gift of God.
Amen.

*A Second Prayer of Gratitude for an Adopted Child
and for All Children*

Thank You, God, for answering our prayers and giving us our child. May we raise her in love. May she grow strong and proud.

Show us, God, how to nurture all her gifts. May we teach her humility and a love of learning. May we lead her to acts of kindness and compassion. May she become a source of blessing to our family, to our world, and to You, God.

Watch over our daughter, God; shield her from all harm. Bless her with health, happiness, and peace. Amen.

Special Needs

Last month, as I was sitting in the waiting room at the clinic where my daughter receives physical, occupational, and speech therapy, a bald, jovial man with rosy cheeks struck up a conversation with me. I had noticed him there before on my visits, but we had never spoken. He told me about his son who cannot speak words but can make only squeaking sounds. I described my daughter's various challenges. I told him how worried I was about her. He looked at me with the delighted smile of the Buddha and said, "I've been watching your daughter for some weeks now, and I want you to know that she is something special. She's got the real thing, that rare quality. She's going to surpass you, she'll put you both to shame—you and your husband. She's going to leave you in the dust. She's going to be so far ahead of you that she will achieve things you won't even be able to dream of. When that day arrives, just remember that I was the one who told you so." My eyes started to tear up. I had been sitting in the waiting room worrying about my daughter, and this extraordinary man transformed my thinking. He delivered a prophecy of hope. Instead of worrying about the future, I needed to start looking forward to it eagerly.

How we think about our children has prophetic implications. If we see our children as damaged, they may come to see themselves that way, and they may be afraid to venture out into the world. If we believe that our children are capable of greatness, they may soon begin to uncover their greatness, to embrace it, and to achieve it.

I wrote this prayer for parents of special needs children. But when I shared these words with my friends and colleagues, they reminded me that the prayer applies to all parents and all children. May we all embrace our children as they are, may all parents be blessed with patience and strength, may all our children be surrounded in love.

A Prayer for a Parent of a Special Needs Child and for All Parents of All Children

Help me, God, to embrace my child as he is. Teach me how to raise him in love and joy and confidence. Show me how to help him realize all the gifts You have placed inside him. Prevent me from pressuring him to become what he can never be or does not want to be. When I find myself mourning for what he is not, open my eyes to the holy blessing that he is. When feelings of jealousy surface toward other parents, soften my heart, open my soul. When my patience wears thin, calm me with Your comforting presence. When I feel as if I have no more to give, be my strength, God, abiding and unending. When I hover over my child too closely, remind me to step back and make room for him to fly. If he should fail, teach me how to encourage him to try again. When others are cruel to him, place words of wisdom and comfort on my tongue and place fortitude in his heart. Help him, God. Watch over him. Protect him from harm. Shield him from frustration and hurt. Fill him with pride, God. Teach him to stand up for himself. Grant him good health. Bless him with true and enduring friends. Nurture his awesome potential, God; let it flourish and become manifest. Let him be happy, God. Surround him with Your love. I thank You, God, for giving me this very child. He is a gift of God, a precious child, a rare soul, a miracle. He is mine. Amen. ✤

 The Right Words

Last year, as I was driving my seven-year-old son, Adi, home from school, he asked me from the backseat, "Mom, what's sex?" I almost hit the car in front of me. I hadn't expected to have this conversation with him quite this early. But there it was, and I knew I had to rise to the occasion. I took a deep breath, gathered my thoughts, and replied, "Sex is when you love someone very much and you want to share your love." "Uh-huh," he said. I drove a few more blocks and added, "Sex is when you love someone very much and you want to *show* your love." "Uh-huh," he said. I drove a few more blocks and added, "Sex is when you love someone very much and you want to show your love with your body." "Uh-huh," he said. I drove a few more blocks and asked, "Adi, what made you ask me about sex? Was somebody talking to you about it today?" He said, "Yeah. We had to fill out this form for soccer camp and it said 'sex' and then there were these two boxes after it."

As a parent you can have all the right answers and still be wrong if you fail to comprehend the question that your child is asking.

A Parent's Prayer for Wisdom

Bless me, God.
Infuse my spirit with patience
and my body with energy.
Send insight to my eyes
and affection to my arms.
Place understanding in my heart
and wisdom on my tongue.
Fill my character with integrity
and my actions with kindness.
May I raise children who will bring blessings to me,
    to all people,
and to You, my God. Amen.

A Prayer for the Parent of a Teenager

My little boy has grown into a man-child. I don't know how to be his father, God. Sometimes he wants me, especially when he needs me. Other times he looks at me with eyes of contempt.

Help me, God. Help me to be patient when he tests me. Steady me when my temper flares. Remind me that he still needs me even when he doesn't want me.

Teach me how to hold him close and let him go, how to protect him from the world and expose him to the world, how to guide him and trust him. Give me strength, God, and confidence, and wisdom.

Watch over him, God. Protect him from those who can lead him astray. Teach him to believe in himself, to have faith in goodness. Give him courage, God, and humility, and happiness, and the love of good friends.

Bless our family, God, with health, with peace, with joy, and with love. Amen.

A Prayer When a Child Is in Trouble

My child is in trouble, God, and I'm not sure what to say to her. She needs me now, and I can't seem to do or say the right thing. Every time I open my mouth we end up in a fight.

I love her more than life, God; I don't mean to push her away. I simply don't know how to help her anymore. When she was small, she would run to me in tears and I could kiss away her hurts. But now her hurts run deep, and she shuts me out.

Help her, God. Save her from the grip of those who are leading her astray. Watch over her, God; protect her from all harm. Turn her heart to me, God; help her see that I am not the enemy. Help me see that she is not my enemy either.

Help me, God. Put insight in my heart and wisdom on my lips. Let me say the right words of guidance.

Bless our family, God; grace us with peace. Amen.

A Prayer for Wisdom for Divorced Parents

We ask for Your wisdom, God, in raising our child after our divorce. Although we live apart, teach us how to work together for her sake. Teach us a way to cooperate with decency, integrity, and honesty. Show us how to determine her custody and future wisely. Remind us to focus on what is best for her and not on what is most convenient for ourselves. Show us how to offer her stability in the midst of this time of instability. Give us the words to reassure her that our love for her will never die, even though our marriage has ended. Fill us with the insight to perceive her needs even when she tries to conceal them. When she is sad or frightened or angry, put wisdom in our hearts, God, and comfort on our lips. When we disagree with each other, save us both from vindictiveness and cruelty, lead us to compromise. Help us, God. Prevent us from using her in any way in order to get back at each other. Shield us from competing for her love. Protect us from spoiling her with presents as a way to compensate for our absence. Instead, let us indulge her with our love; let us shower her with our caring. Give us the strength, God, to collaborate with dignity and grace in honor of the life we once shared, and in reverence for the child we will forever share. Bless us, God, with health, with joy, and with peace. Amen.

A Prayer to Say When Your Child Grows Up and Moves Out

I've known for some time that this day was coming; now it is here. How did time pass me by so quickly? I wish I would have made better use of each day that my son was home with me. I wish I could take back all the times I was too busy to be with him.

I know that the goal of a parent is to raise a child to become independent. But I'm not ready. I'm not ready to let him go. I will miss him so much.

Help me, God. Heal my loneliness. Help me send him off with a full heart. Help me work through my pain. Help me find new fulfillment in my life.

Bless him, God. Bless the choices he makes. Bless the path he takes. Bless his labors. Bless his heart with love, his actions with kindness, and his words with wisdom.

Watch over him, God, always. Amen. ✒

Blessing Our Parents

It was my mother's seventy-fifth birthday, and our family and many dear friends gathered to celebrate with her. My mom was surrounded by love. There was music, and there were presents, and of course there was a cake. At the point when everyone was expecting my mother to say a few words, she turned to me and said, "Nomi, I'd like you to bless me." There have certainly been many times in my life when I have thanked my mother, and many times that I've told her how much I love her. But it never occurred to me to bless her. I was so moved by this request. When I stood up, placed my hands on my mother's head, and blessed her, I cannot describe the feelings that passed between us. All I can say is, bless your parents. You won't regret it. You will never forget it.

A Blessing for Children to Say to Their Parents

You gave me my life. You give me your wisdom, your guidance, your concern, your love. You are my mentor, my protector, my moral compass, my comfort. There are no words to express my gratitude for all the blessings you have given me. Still, I tell you, thank you.

May God bless you as you have blessed me, with life, with health, with joy, and with love. Amen.

FIVE

Prayers for Healing

None of us is a stranger to disappointment. Family members let us down; friends forsake us. But when you fall ill, it is your own body that fails you. Realizing that you cannot count upon your body to do its job properly is frightening. You turn to doctors hoping they can discover the source of your ailment and restore you to health. Placing your life in the hands of another is an act of faith. You pray that your doctor will be patient and wise and thorough. In your vulnerability, you hope you will not be deceived, mistreated, or ignored.

It is true that illness leads to fear. But illness can also lead to faith. There is no house of worship greater than a hospital. It is the sanctuary for the sick and the suffering. God is on call twenty-four hours a day. Prayers rise up and intermingle. A woman in labor cries, "Save me, God." A medical student asks, "Help me make the correct diagnosis, God." A man awakes from surgery and says, "I am grateful to be alive, God." A young girl sits on the floor in the hallway and prays, "Please, God, I want my mother to come home." A patient receiving chemotherapy beseeches, "Please, God, make these treatments work." A young husband and wife look down at the newborn child nestled in their arms and whisper, "Thank You, God."

Do these prayers work? Is God listening? I believe that God hears us whenever we call. God is with us. We are never alone. God hears even the silent prayers that no ear can hear. And God answers us. But we should not confuse prayer with magic. When we pray, we connect with God's power. It may not be power enough to cure all illnesses, but it is power enough to help us fight for our lives.

Those "faith healers" on television who claim to perform instant miracles with the touch of a hand prey upon the vulnerable and offer nothing but false hope. God's healing gives us true hope.

God's healing is found in a scientist's devotion to curing disease. God's healing comes when a dying person who feared death finds the power to embrace it instead. God's healing is in the love of family, the compassion of friends, the selfless acts of complete strangers. God's healing is the strength that lies within us, the courage to fight, the determination to prevail against overwhelming odds. God's healing is at work when we overcome our fears, when we reach out to help one another, when we refuse to give in to despair.

Illness and Fear

It is natural to be frightened when we become ill. We feel vulnerable. We worry; we want to know that everything will turn out all right. We sometimes feel alone even when loved ones are by our side. The illness lies within us, and no one else knows exactly how we feel. Prayer has the power to transform our fear into faith. It reminds us that we are never alone. Everything we are, body and soul, is in the hand of God, whose presence fills the universe and who is as close to us as our own breath. No matter what this unpredictable world sends our way, with God by our side we can find the strength to confront our fears. So pray and welcome God's healing power.

A Prayer for Healing

I am sick, God. And I am frightened. I feel so alone. I am scared of doctors. I am scared of pain and uncertainty, of feeling helpless.

Be with me, God. Be there when others fail me. Be my strength and my protector. Be my friend.

Hear me, God. Heal me, God. Lead me back to strength, God, back to health, back to life, back to You. Amen.

A Blessing for Healing
FOR PHYSICAL AND SPIRITUAL HEALING
THAT CAN BE SAID WITH THE LAYING ON OF HANDS

May God heal you, body and soul.
May your pain cease,
May your strength increase,
May your fears be released,
May blessings, love, and joy surround you.
Amen.

A Prayer Before Surgery

I am scared, God. I feel vulnerable. I don't like feeling helpless. I am worried. So before my surgery I pray:

I place my body and soul in Your hands. Please watch over me, God, in the operating room. Stay beside me. Never leave me. Strengthen my will to live. Enlighten my doctors and nurses with the skill, wisdom, and insight to mend and cure me properly. Let this procedure go smoothly without complication. Watch over my loved ones who are worrying about me now. Remind me that I am resilient. That I can and will grow stronger each day. Bless me, God, with Your healing power, protect me from all harm, shield me from pain. And when I wake, God, give me the courage and passion to fight for the sacred treasure You have granted me: my life. Amen. ✍

A Prayer to Say When a Loved One Is in Surgery

God, watch over _____ during her surgery. Stay beside her. Protect her. Shield her from fear and pain. Bless her doctors and nurses with wisdom and strength. May they bring us good news.

Spread Your healing power over _____. Return her to us, God, whole and strong. Amen. ✍

A Prayer After Surgery

Thank You, God. Thank You for my life. Thank You for seeing me through. Thank You for this wondrous new day. Thank You for tomorrow's hope, for the miracle of medicine and the skills of my doctors and nurses, for the power to heal and grow, for the gift of a new beginning. Amen. ✍

———

A Prayer for Loved Ones to Recite After Surgery

Thank You, God. _____ has safely emerged from surgery. Thank You for restoring him to us, for turning our fear into joy.

Bless _____ with Your healing light. Watch over him, God; protect him from all harm. Help him to recover quickly. May he grow stronger and stronger each day. Amen. ✍

A Healer's Prayer
FOR PHYSICIANS AND FOR ALL HEALERS

Open my eyes, God; let no symptom of illness elude me.

Steady my hands, God; shield me from fear, anxiety, and impatience. Teach me to breathe deeply, to find peace, calm, and clarity in even the most stressful situations.

Open my heart, God; remind me that my compassion is as essential as my precision.

Open my mind, God; shelter me from distraction, bless me with insight, curiosity, and the humility to ask for help.

Open my arms, God; remind me that even when I have no cure to offer, precious healing resides in the touch of my hands.

Open my mouth, God; place wisdom on my tongue, bless me with words that are clear and kind, honest and encouraging.

Open my ears, God; teach me to listen with my entire being.

When I am overwhelmed and exhausted, when I feel as if I have no more to give, be my strength, God, renew my spirit, revive my soul.

I am humbled by the miracles that unfold before me each day: miracles of nature, miracles of medicine, miracles of the human spirit, miracles that lie beyond my comprehension.

I thank You, God, for entrusting me with this sacred calling. Amen. ✄

A Prayer for Those Who Tend to the Sick

I don't get paid much, thanked much, or noticed much. But I am here, and I know how valuable I am. I am the one who stays when everyone else goes home. I clean things no one else will touch. I watch things no one else can bear to see. I bring comfort and companionship. I listen, I hear.

I pray to You, God, for strength. When I grow weary, renew my spirit. When my patience wears thin, bless me with stamina. When I feel forgotten and alone, show me that You are near. When others treat me poorly, remind me that I am doing Your work.

I thank You, God, for giving me the opportunity to bring light into the lives of the afflicted. Amen. ✍

A Prayer When a Child Is Ill

My child is in need of Your healing powers, God. I am frightened. Help me be strong. Let me not show him my fear.

He is my life, God. Please heal him. Make him strong, make him well. Send wisdom and compassion to his doctors and nurses.

Watch over him, God, protect him. Heal him, God; please hear me, God. Return him to me in health, in strength, and in blessing. Amen.

Living with Disability

Not long ago a mother called me. Her son had recently celebrated his tenth birthday. When he blew out the candles on his cake, she asked him what he had wished for. He replied, "I wished that God would let me walk." The mother was heartbroken for her son. If only she could do something to take away his pain and frustration. How could she explain to him why God was not going to give him back the use of his legs.

Every disability is an obstacle placed in our path. Sometimes we dream of what life would be without that barrier. We don't want to be different. We long to be free, to approach the world with the ease that others do. But every disability is also a teacher. When there is a hurdle in our way, we have to learn to be creative, we have to find a way around it, we have to seek out an alternate route. I told the mother I believe God gives us strength to flourish in every situation we are in. She said to me, "I know. God didn't give my son legs for walking; God gave him wings to fly. I have to help him find his wings."

A Prayer for Living with Disability

God, I wish I could pray and You would magically free me from disability. I wish I were not handed this fate. But the only life I have is the one You have given me.

Help me, God, to realize all the gifts hidden inside me. Teach me that there is a way around each obstacle, that I can surmount each barrier in my path. Shield me, God, from stares and cruelty. Most of all, protect me from pity. I don't want people's pity, I want their companionship, their respect, their love.

When I grow weary, God, renew my spirit. When I am frightened, teach me faith. When I despair, fill me with hope. When I get frustrated, be my comfort. Remind me to treasure all the miracles that I often ignore.

Bless me, God, with life and strength and joy. Amen.

A Prayer When One Is Undergoing a Long and Draining Treatment

I'm tired, God. My doctors say that this treatment will help me, but it is sapping me of my strength. I'm sick of feeling sick, God. Sometimes I want to give up. But most of the time I just want to get better.

I love being outdoors and breathing fresh air. I love the sun and the rain. I love the sky at night. I love my family and friends.

I love life, God. I love it more now than ever before. Please, God, let me keep it. Help me to bear the stench of medicines and hospitals. Give me the stamina to stare down this disease and conquer it.

Fill me with strength, God, and I will fight for my life. Fill me with health, God, that I may live. Amen.

Battling Breast Cancer

Last year I spoke about healing at a conference for breast cancer survivors sponsored by the American Cancer Society. The room was filled with women of all races and faiths who shared a common bond: their struggle against breast cancer.

One woman stood up and said that the word "survivor" applied to anyone who faced death and somehow managed to remain alive. She preferred to call herself and all her companions "veterans." She proclaimed that a veteran is someone who has fought a battle. And all the women present had certainly fought fiercely and courageously. Then she added, "Veterans remember their fallen comrades, and we too will forever remember our fallen." Then we observed a moment of silence in memory of all the women who had lost their lives in the battle against breast cancer.

I had been asked to talk about healing, but at that moment as I looked around the room, I felt that I had so much to *learn* about healing from these brave and passionate women.

I spoke about sources of comfort and strength and about the healing power of prayer. Then I encouraged each person present to write a prayer. One by one, those who wished to stood up to share their words to God. The room grew perfectly still. It was a moment of pure transcendence. Even the waiters and busboys stood still to listen. There were expressions of fear and of faith, of anger and of gratitude, of frustration and of triumph, of vulnerability and of boundless strength.

A great healing enveloped us all.

A Prayer for Healing from Breast Cancer

When I think of breasts, I think of life. A mother suckling her infant, her breasts filled with sweet milk. When I think of breasts, I think of pleasure. The rapture of two bodies entwined in love. But this breast of mine is filled with disease. It's not right, God. It's not fair. I am angry. And I am frightened, God. I want to live. I am prepared to trade my breast for the promise of life. I am prepared to lose a part of my breast, my whole breast, both of my breasts. I am prepared to undergo radiation, chemotherapy, experimental trials, whatever treatments my doctors deem necessary to restore me to health. Help me, God. Fill me with the strength and the stamina to fight for my life. Calm my fears. Show me that I am whole and holy and beautiful and desirable. Remind me, God, that I am loved, that I am powerful, that I am not alone. Let the scars in my soul heal along with those in my body. Heal me, God; hear me, God; be with me, God. Amen.

A Prayer When Life Is Hanging in the Balance

My doctors are telling me that things don't look too good. I'm scared, God. Help me, God. Give me hope. Give me something to fight for. Send me a miracle, God. Let me be the one who beats the odds.

I used to take each morning for granted. I would complain about this and that. But now I know that every blessed moment is a miracle.

Let me make every moment count. Let me enjoy the love of my family. Let me forgive others and ask for their forgiveness as well. Give me dignity, God, throughout the coming struggle.

Watch over me, God; protect me, heal me. Let me live, God. Amen. ✎

Overcoming Addiction

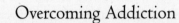

Many people who fall prey to the disease of addiction experience a void in their lives. They feel empty, alone, unloved, abandoned, cut off. They try to satisfy this hunger through drugs, alcohol, sex, food, gambling, shopping, even work. But the emptiness still remains. And as the addiction deepens, so does the void. No drug, no food, no job, no amount of money is ever going to fill this vacuum. Many of us keep making the same mistake over and over again. We keep feeding our bodies when it is our souls that need nourishment.

Each day, each year we spend in addiction, we get more and more cut off from our souls and from our real source of comfort. Our souls grow hungrier and weaker by the day. You can drink yourself into oblivion but never quench your thirst. You can continue along this futile path, or you can start addressing the deeper hunger. The soul's longing is for God, the Source of all souls. Our souls seek to speak to God.

When we pray, we begin to sense God's presence in all things. We remember that we are not alone. We learn that a silent thread of holiness connects all of us to each other and to God. That is why twelve-step programs like Alcoholics Anonymous have been so effective at treating addiction. They urge people to stop hiding from themselves and to start searching their souls. They create a community where people feel welcome and understood. They insist that forming a relationship with God, or a higher power, is the key to achieving sobriety. Of course, prayer is not a cure for addiction, but when we pray we can receive the strength we need to fight the long and difficult battle that lies before us.

If you have been deceiving yourself, if you have been denying your addiction, it is time to stop trying to muffle the sound of your soul. Seek out a treatment program that can help you. And bring your hunger to God.

If you have been hiding your addiction from others, if you believe there is a darkness within you that no one can understand, remember that God knows you. You don't need to conceal anything.

We can put on a front with anyone in our lives. We can pretend that all is well, that we are okay. But there's no way to deceive God. Before God, we are all naked. Our secrets are exposed. And that's frightening.

It's natural to want to hide. But God is calling out to us. God is hoping we will find the strength to live up to the best in ourselves. The choice is ours. We can hide or we can turn to God in all our nakedness, in all our frailty.

We have to remember that to stand before a God who knows all our secrets is not *just* frightening. It is also deeply comforting. It means that no matter how false our lives may feel, we are known, we are understood, and we are loved.

A Prayer to Combat Addiction

God, I have an addiction. It is hurting me and those I love. I am frightened. Be with me, God, calm my fears, show me Your love.

Give me the courage to conquer my cravings. Grant me the strength to stay far from temptations and from people who can lead me astray. Keep me far from any comfort that is false and destructive.

Help me, God, to hear the cry of my soul. Teach me that I have the power to remake my life, to repair what I have destroyed, to recover what I have lost, to receive all the blessings I have ignored.

When I fall into despair, fill me with hope. If I stray from my path, show me how to begin again. Renew my faith in myself, God, teach me to love myself. Show me how to vanquish the darkness in my heart and uncover the pure, holy light that shines inside me. Open my eyes to all the miracles that surround me.

Bless my journey, God; lead me on the path back to life, back to love, back to You. Amen.

A Prayer for Spiritual Healing from Depression

I remember joy, God, but I can't feel it anymore. Everything seems hopeless and tiresome. I think I've lost my soul. All I have left is this dreary hollow body. The people who love me are trying to help, but I can't seem to find my way out of this darkness.

Free me, God. Breathe a new spirit into me. Give me strength. Give me patience. Give me hope. Be with me. Lead me back to joy, back to love, back to life, back to You. Amen.

A Prayer of Thanks for Healing

I thought You had forgotten me. I felt abandoned and alone. I prayed to You, but You never answered. I searched, but I couldn't find You. And then, without warning, You spread Your love over me and taught me not to fear. You quieted me, You healed me, You blessed me, You stretch Your comfort over all living things.

Thank You, God, for giving me life and for saving my life. Amen.

SIX

Work Prayers

What do you want to be when you grow up? is a question we ask of all children. From the youngest age we prepare them for the fact that one day they will need to get a job. When we are young, we have romantic ideas about what we will become. Our parents entertain these fanciful hopes as well. They dream that their children will turn out to be exceptional, gifted, famous. But as we grow, reality sets in and our options begin to diminish. You learn that you will never be a concert pianist, a ballerina, a basketball star, or the president of the United States. Sooner or later life forces you to choose. For most of us, work is rarely a glamorous endeavor. Even so-called glamorous work is rarely glamorous. Finding fulfilling work is no easy task. When you land such a job, retaining your enthusiasm from day to day is still quite a challenge. Every job has its negative components: office politics; competition between coworkers; differences of opinion with your boss; a desire for better pay, better hours, a nicer work space; personality differences; the fear of losing your job; the dues you must pay to get ahead.

But as difficult as work can sometimes be, it is also a privilege. It is a gift to be healthy, to earn a living, to be able to support ourselves and our loved ones. Through our work we are contributing to our society and our world. No matter what our position, we have the opportunity to make life a little better for someone else. No matter how tedious our task may seem, we each have the capacity to find joy and satisfaction in our efforts. And if work becomes unbearable, we are fortunate to live in this great country where we are free to strive for new possibilities.

We have the power to turn every day into a meaningful day. We are blessed with talent and potential and creativity. But too often we take these blessings for granted and allow ourselves to sink into complacency and boredom. Every morning God gives us a new opportunity to recover our passion and realize our dreams.

A Prayer for Meaning, Integrity, and Passion at Work

God, inspire me to transform my career into a calling. Help me to rekindle the flame of passion that once burned so brightly. Teach me how to turn my labor into meaning and deep satisfaction.

Give me the insight to think in new ways, the confidence to trust my instincts, the humility to learn from those who are wiser and more experienced. May I find the courage to stand up for what I believe. May I never compromise my integrity in order to get ahead.

Remind me, God, to treat my colleagues and subordinates with patience, kindness, and respect. Give me the strength to overcome the envy and resentments that poison my soul and my relationships.

Most of all, I pray that my work be a reflection of Your will, that I can help to bring goodness into this world. Amen.

A Blessing for a Business

Bless my business, God. Let it take root and flourish. Bless my labors with success. Shield me, God, from greed and envy. Help me to conduct all my transactions in honesty. Let my courage and creativity flow freely. Let my worries subside.

Teach me, God, how to balance my work and my family. Show me how to make time for work and for rest. Most of all, I pray that my work be a reflection of Your will, that I can help to bring goodness into this world. Amen.

A Big Challenge

One year, when I was a congregational rabbi, on the night before Yom Kippur, I fell asleep and had the following dream. I was standing on the pulpit in front of my congregation. The sanctuary was packed; people were standing in the aisles. A hush fell over the crowd as I was about to speak. I looked down at the lectern, and my heart started to race. My sermon was gone. All I found was a pile of long narrow strips of paper. I picked one up; it read "$1.99, $3.74, $5.69 . . ." The strips of paper were grocery store receipts. I turned one receipt over, and, to my surprise, I found words from my sermon printed on the back. By this time my congregants were whispering and grumbling. I was shaking and sweating. Every receipt I turned over had some piece of my sermon on it. But the strips were all out of order. Nothing I read made any sense. Then I woke up. And I savored that overwhelming rush of relief that envelops you when you realize your nightmare was only a dream. Just the same, that year I must have printed out about ten copies of my sermon, which I stashed at strategic locations all over the pulpit.

YOU ARE A SPRING

The Talmud offers this story about rising to a challenge. Rabbi Eliezer was a young disciple of the great sage Rabbi Johanan ben Zakkai. One day, in the presence of all the great scholars, Johanan asked Eliezer to teach. Eliezer began to panic. He said, "I have nothing to teach because I am like a well that can't bring forth new water. All I know is what you have taught me. I have nothing new to say." But Johanan turned to his frightened student and said, "You are not a stagnant well, you are a spring that is forever bringing forth new water." With those words of encouragement Eliezer stood and offered up insights that no ear had ever heard before. His face began to shine like the sun. When Eliezer was done speaking, his mentor, Johanan, stood up, walked toward Eliezer, and kissed him on the head with pride and love.

Sometimes we feel like imposters. We worry that we cannot possibly rise to the challenge that lies before us. But we are mistaken. When feelings of panic overtake you, remember Rabbi Johanan's words of encouragement. You are a spring that is forever renewing itself. Gather up your confidence and take on your challenge. Let your face shine, and let your creativity flow.

A Prayer Before a Big Challenge

Help me, God. Let me succeed. Teach me to believe that I can rise to this occasion.

Calm my fears. Show me how to put this ordeal into perspective. Remind me that it is not a matter of life and death but merely a challenge—a challenge that I have the capacity to meet head-on. Instead of fearing this test, help me, God, to view it as an opportunity to stretch and learn and grow.

Let my anxiety give way to assurance; let my scattered thoughts give way to focused attention; let my fears give way to faith.

Be with me, God; release the tension that binds me; free me so that I can shine. Amen. ✒

A Prayer for Creativity

I know you have placed inspiration inside of me, God, but I don't always know how to retrieve it. There are so many obstacles that stand in my way. Sometimes I have a revelation that comes to me easily like a gift from heaven. But most of the time I have to struggle and sweat to uncover a single original thought.

Help me, God. Teach me to be still long enough to experience the depth of my own imagination. Remind me that I cannot force a breakthrough; I have to open myself up, body and soul, so that I can receive the insight I have been praying for. Free me, God, from fears that blind my vision.

May my creativity flow, may I produce a thing of beauty, God, that will adorn Your world.

Thank You, God, for filling me with Your light; bless You, Source of all creation. Amen. ✒

A Prayer for Overcoming Burnout

I am weary, God; please renew my spirit.
When I despair, fill me with hope.
When I feel as if I have no more to give, remind
   me that my strength comes from You.
When I assume that my energy is finite, teach me
   to see that I am connected to an infinite source
   of inspiration and goodness.
When I lose faith in myself, remind me that I am
   blessed with enormous talent and ability.
When I get lazy, remind me that there is much
   work to be done and that there are many
   people who need my assistance. Teach me to
   see that my efforts do make a difference.
When I forget why I am doing what I am doing,
   help me to recover the excitement, the meaning, and the satisfaction that led me to this
   work.
When I lose direction, show me the way, God,
   back to passion, back to enthusiasm, back to
   You. Amen.

A Prayer to Overcome Excessive Competitiveness

I've always been a competitive person, God, but I fear I've gone too far. I've grown selfish, God. I've neglected my family. I've wished for my colleagues to fail. I've rejoiced at their ruin. I have refused to offer help when my help was needed.

Help me, God. Teach me that there is goodness inside me. Show me how to harness my drive and direct it toward honorable ambitions. Let me become driven for causes that bring healing to Your world. Teach me, God, to see that success is not an end in itself.

Fill me with Your peace, God, so that I can slow down and rejoice in all the blessings that surround me. Amen.

An Unemployment Prayer

I've lost my job, God, and I feel like a failure. I wasn't prepared for the shame, the humiliation, the anger, the blow to my confidence. I didn't see it coming. I feel so naked.

I never realized this before, but having a job is like wearing clothing. It makes you feel safe, protected. But being unemployed is like standing naked in front of everyone you know. Someone asks you, "What do you do?" and you feel like hiding. People start pitying you and whispering about you.

I'm scared, God. My family can't survive without my income. We're in debt and now there's no way to climb out of the hole we've dug.

Help me, God. Fill me with courage and strength. Restore the faith I used to have in myself. Remind me that I am talented and capable and energetic and loyal.

Steady my nerves, God; calm my fears. Save me from self-pity. Lead me on the path toward a new opportunity, a new hope, a new beginning. Amen.

A Prayer for a Career Change

Life is short, God; I want to make a change. I am unhappy in my work, God. It's hard to invest so much time in something unfulfilling. I'd like to try something new, but I'm frightened. I'm scared of the financial strain this will put on my family. I'm worried about what people will say.

Help me, God. Give me the strength to make this leap. Fill me with courage and with the stamina I will need to see this through. Let the disapproval of others not hinder me in my quest.

Be with me, God, along this difficult journey. When the obstacles seem insurmountable, fill me with hope and persistence. When I begin to doubt myself, fill me with faith. When I lose my way, God, be my guide on the road to meaning, pride, and deep satisfaction. Amen.

A Prayer Before a Job Interview

I really want this job, God; I need this job. Help me, God. Teach me to believe in myself, to see that I am qualified for this position. Calm my fears, God; soothe my nerves. Let me enter this interview with assurance and confidence. Let me speak my mind; let my thoughts flow freely.

Remind me not only to talk but to listen. Show me how to impress without seeming pompous, how to be agreeable without seeming ingratiating, how to be enthusiastic without seeming desperate.

Be with me, God; fill me with strength and faith and light. Let me shine today, God. Amen.

SEVEN

Prayers for Comfort and Strength in Difficult Times

As I mentioned earlier, many people feel uncomfortable praying to God when they are in pain because they have never approached God before. They feel hypocritical, or unworthy, or ashamed. They worry that God will say, "Look who's come crawling back to me now!" But God isn't petty, and God isn't a stranger. I believe that, whether we know it or not, we have been in a relationship with God all along. God is with us during our moments of triumph and during our moments of sorrow as well. God is not looking to add to our suffering in a time of pain. God is here to offer comfort, strength, light. So talk to God, shout out in anger, show your fears, share your pain, ask for help. You are not alone. Reach out to people, they may surprise you. God may answer you through them.

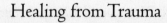

Healing from Trauma

There are thousands upon thousands of people who have been traumatized by crime. It's difficult to put these horrible experiences behind us. It's natural to be shaken to our cores. Memories invade our thoughts. Fears can sometimes paralyze us. But along with the memory of the nightmare there is also a deep gratitude for having survived.

The challenge for anyone who has endured trauma is learning how to separate the present from the past. Can we learn to live without crippling fear? Can we find the strength to trust again? Can we embrace all the blessings that surround us?

A Prayer for a Victim of Crime

I am scared, God. I feel so vulnerable and exposed. Why did this have to happen, God? Why didn't You protect me? What is wrong with this world?

Be with me, God; let me know You are near. Fill me with strength and courage. Return me to confidence, God; let me feel secure again. I don't want to live in fear anymore. I don't want to feel like a victim anymore.

When the nightmare of what I experienced invades my thoughts, calm my fears, God; remind me that I am safe now, and that I am fortunate to be alive. I am grateful, God, for my life, for my family, for my health.

God, please obstruct the plans of any person plotting to do harm to another.

Watch over us, God; watch over Your world. Shelter us all with peace. Amen. ✘

Isolation and Self-Pity

It is natural to turn inward when sorrow comes. We need time alone to digest the awful reality that we must now face. But we have to be careful not to create a wall around us so thick that no one can penetrate it. When people isolate themselves, they begin to lose perspective. Despair sets in, and so do envy and self-pity. We have to muster up all of our strength to reach out to the community of family and friends who are ready to offer comfort and companionship.

A Prayer for the Strength to Combat Self-Pity

When I am feeling self-pity, God, help me to see beyond myself.

When I am feeling despair, restore me to hope.

When I shut people out, help me to believe in the healing power of companionship. Remind me that I am not alone, that I am needed, that I am heard, that I am loved.

And that You are with me, now and always. Amen.

A Prayer to Combat Envy

Soften my hardened heart, God. In my suffering I have grown callous and unforgiving. Secretly, I have been wishing for my friends to fall. But this envy of mine is causing me to fall.

Teach me, God, to cherish all that I am, all that I have, all that I have yet to offer. Help me to rejoice in the joy of others even when in pain, to take pleasure in their pleasure, to wish them nothing but blessings and peace. Amen.

A Prayer to Subdue Guilt

I've been blaming myself, God, for the tragedy that has befallen me. The thoughts keep running through my mind: I *could* have done more. I *should* have done more. But none of this self-doubt can erase the past.

Teach me, God, to believe that I don't deserve to be punished forever. Help me to forgive and to love myself despite my weakness.

Show me Your love, this day and always. Amen.

Bouncing Back

Eventually life tests us all. There isn't a human being alive who has not faced defeat. The question that we must all ask ourselves is not: How are we to avoid pain? But rather: When sorrow comes, how can we muster the resources to *recover* from pain? No one would ever wish misfortune upon themselves. But suffering is a great teacher. It teaches us empathy, compassion, and wisdom. Most of all, it forces us to learn that we are far stronger than we ever suspected.

A Prayer for the Power to Return from the Depths of Sorrow

Teach me always to believe in my power to return to life, to hope, and to You, God, no matter what pains I have endured, no matter how far I have strayed from You. Give me the strength to resurrect my weary spirit. Revive me, God, so I can embrace life once more in joy, in passion, in peace. Amen.

A Prayer for Resilience

Please, God, help me to recognize my strength. May I always remember that no matter how far I have fallen, no matter how bleak my life may seem, no matter how lost I may feel, that I can always begin again. Amen.

———

A Prayer Asking God to Put an End to One's Suffering

I am tired of waiting, God. I have suffered for too long and I am beginning to lose hope. I turn to You now, God, to put an end to this agony of mine. If relief is not near, give me the patience and the strength to continue to dwell in the darkness, to face this time of suffering with courage and dignity and faith.

Be my light, God; illuminate my way. Lead me to joy and healing and peace. Amen.

Confronting What We Must Face

We are only human. When difficulties arise, we naturally look for ways to avoid them. We seek out distractions, we look for ways to ignore or deny reality. But unfortunately, closing our eyes does not improve our situation, nor does it heal our pain. When we refuse to confront a problem, it only festers and grows.

One way to break the cycle of avoidance is to embrace silence. Instead of hiding from our pain, we must be still enough to actually experience it. Only then can we begin the process of repair. In silence we may uncover answers that had been available to us all along. In silence God speaks to us.

Embracing Silence
A PRAYER FOR THE STRENGTH TO STOP
RUNNING FROM PAIN

God who speaks in silence, teach me not to fear silence. Remind me that running from pain only causes more pain, that distraction is no cure for suffering. Give me the courage to embrace the stillness, to encounter the quiet, that I might learn to hear Your holy voice. Amen. ✘

———

A Prayer to Face What We Have Been Denying

God, I have been running and hiding, and I am weary. Help me to face the awful truth that I can no longer deny. Remind me that ignoring my pain will never make it disappear. Give me the courage to confront what I have so feared, the strength to endure what I cannot escape.

Be with me. Guide me. Never forsake me. Amen. ✘

When God Lets Us Down

I used to think God was Superman. I assumed that whenever we prayed, God would magically swoop down to protect good people and punish bad ones. It is this depiction of God that often leads us to feel angry with God when we get hurt. We feel abandoned and neglected. We conclude that prayer is a waste of time. But experience has taught me that prayer is rarely that direct. I know now that God is not Superman. God does not always protect innocent people from harm. Instead, I have come to believe in a God who is neither a man nor a woman, a God who lives not in heaven but everywhere. A God who answers our prayers not by preventing terrible things from happening but by being beside us and filling us with strength and hope and love through good and bad times.

There was a time when I hated God for not answering my prayers, but my hate has given way to determination, to hope, to awe, and to love. I have learned how to start praying again. Not the prayers of my youth when I expected God to save my world, when I thought I had the power to control my fate. But the prayers of someone who takes God as a given but God's actions as a mystery. I haven't stopped making requests. But I *have* stopped expecting automatic and predictable responses to my petitions.

Now I pray for strength and wisdom. When I pray to God to heal the sick, to eradicate war, poverty, and disaster, I know full well that I am asking for things that are humanity's responsibility, not God's. But I hope that God will give human beings the compassion, the courage, and the insight to repair and heal our world.

I also turn to God to simply offer praise and thanks. I pray because prayer strengthens me; it reminds me to take nothing for granted; it challenges me to strive for better. I pray because I have the *need* to pray. I have the desire to tell God my deepest fears and hopes, to articulate my innermost feelings and thoughts. I pray because I long to share secrets that I may never share with anyone else, because I believe that God hears and understands. I pray because talking to God heals me.

A Prayer When We Feel That God Has Let Us Down

When I was in trouble, I prayed to You, God, but You did not shield me from pain. Ever since then I've been unable to pray. Why should I plead for what You cannot or will not provide? Why should I talk when there is no One who will listen? It's embarrassing, humiliating, infuriating. And yet here I am talking to You once more. I no longer seek miracles from You, God. I ask only this: Be with me in my suffering. Amen. ✒

A Prayer for Returning to God
After Enduring a Difficult Time

God, I need to know that You are with me, that You hear my cry. I long to feel Your presence not just this day, but every day. When I am weak and in pain, I need to know You are beside me. That in itself is often comfort enough.

I do not pretend to know Your ways, to know why this world You have created can be so beautiful, so magnificent, and yet so harsh, so ugly, and so full of hate.

The lot You have bestowed upon me is a heavy one. I am angry. I want to know why: why the innocent must suffer, why life is so full of grief.

There are times when I want to have nothing to do with You. When to think of You brings nothing but confusion and ambivalence.

And there are times, like this time, when I seek to return to You, when I feel the emptiness that comes when I am far from You.

Watch over me and my loved ones. Forgive me for all that I have not been. Help me to appreciate all that I have and to realize all that I have to offer.

Help me to find my way back to You so that I may never feel alone. Amen.

Last year I offered a course in pastoral counseling at a rabbinical seminary. In this class I taught rabbis how to extend wisdom and strength to those who come to them in need. One thing I made sure to tell my students was to be aware of situations that lie beyond their realm of expertise. Every spiritual counselor needs to know when to direct an individual to seek the care of a mental health professional. Sometimes an appropriate referral is the best help a religious leader can provide.

I offer similar advice to therapists. Many people seek out psychological or psychiatric help for spiritual problems. They feel isolated and alone. They believe God has let them down. They are mourning the loss of a loved one or plagued with guilt or overcome with temptation. They are overwhelmed with grief. Their trust has been betrayed. They are jealous, angry, hurt. They want to repair a relationship that has grown cold. They long for meaning in their lives. They want to be heard, known, understood. They want someone who will listen and who will free them from the sense of separateness that is the source of so much pain.

In our daily lives we are so often misunderstood. We

carry thoughts within us that no one knows, hopes that have never been voiced, confessions that are too terrible to speak of, yearnings that are too deep to share with even those who are closest to us. I wish more therapists would say to their clients, "It might help you to speak to a member of the clergy about this." Or maybe they could say, "It might help you to talk to God about this." If they did, perhaps thousands upon thousands of people would begin to see that they are not alone. They might come to understand that there is a God who hears us, who knows us intimately, who understands our suffering. A God who accepts us in all our frailty, in all our need, in all our failings. A God who not only sees us as we are, but who sees what we have the potential to become. A God who can comfort us, who can offer us strength and healing and hope.

When members of the clergy offer spiritual counsel to people in need, they pray with them and pray for them; they encourage them to talk to God from their hearts in their own words. They give them rituals to perform and prayers to go home with to say morning and night. They invite them to enter a religious community where they will be welcomed and where their joys and pains and prayers are shared. Soon the same individual who felt isolated and alone begins to feel sheltered from above and embraced from below.

A Prayer to Be Heard

Help me, God, I can no longer hold my suffering inside. I feel so isolated and alone. I don't know whom to turn to, whom to rely on.

Give me the courage, God, to trust someone enough to open my heart. Fill me with the faith that I will not be rejected. Please, God, show me how to find the right person to receive my words. Let it not be someone who will judge me or misunderstand me.

And when there is no one who will listen, hear me, God. Hear me and heal me. Amen.

Losing a Pet

A dying man once told me he hoped he would be reunited with his dog in heaven. He said it just wouldn't be heaven without his dog.

Martin Buber, the great religious philosopher, said all relationships fall into one of two categories: I-it, or I-Thou. An I-it relationship is when we treat others as things, when we value them for their utility. An I-Thou relationship is when we truly experience others and embrace them in all their magnificence. When we achieve this profound contact with another, we get a glimpse of God. Buber insisted that we have the capacity to greet all of nature as a Thou. One of Buber's earliest I-Thou encounters was with a horse. When he was a child, Buber would regularly steal away to feed a certain dapple-grey horse. As he stroked its neck and glorious mane, an overwhelming sense of connection flowed between the boy and the horse. The horse was no longer a stranger, or an other; it had become a Thou.

Many of us have formed deep and powerful bonds with animals who have become true and faithful companions. Losing a pet is not the same as losing a person, but we do need to take the time to mourn our loss.

A Prayer When a Beloved Pet Dies

You were my good friend. We never had a single conversation, but we understood each other. I still keep thinking you'll be there waiting for me when I open the door. The house is empty without you. I miss you more than others could ever understand.

I thank you for being my companion in times of joy, and my comfort in times of pain. I was fortunate to have you in my life and I know your life with me was a happy one.

I will remember you with joy and a smile. May God bless you. Amen.

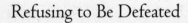

Refusing to Be Defeated

We have only limited power to choose our fate. Horrible things can happen to us at any time. But we all do have the power to choose our response to that fate. We can allow adversity to crush our spirits, fill us with fear, and harden our hearts. Or we can learn from our pain, we can uncover our strength, we can refuse to be defeated.

A Prayer to Find Meaning in Suffering

I am hurting, God. I feel lost, helpless, and alone. My tragedy seems so senseless. Help me, God, to embrace what I cannot understand, to find meaning in my suffering. Remind me that though I am powerless to choose my fate, I hold the power to choose a response to my fate.

May I never be defeated. May I never grow bitter. May my sorrow lead me to strength, to wisdom, to compassion, to You. Amen.

Our Scars Are Our Teachers

There is no such thing as a perfect healing. Our scars will remain with us always. There are two ways to approach the scars that remain within us. We can despise them and look upon them as signs of weakness. Or we can treasure them and learn from them. We can find the strength to turn our curses into blessings, to transform our suffering into wisdom and compassion.

A Prayer for Learning from Pain

My wounds may heal, God, but my scars may never fade. Help me to embrace them, not despise them. Teach me how to live with my scars, how to tend to them, how to learn from them.

Remind me that I have the power to turn my curses into blessings, my shame into pride, my sadness into strength, my pain into compassion. Amen.

———

A Prayer for Comfort and Strength

When I feel tainted, God, remind me that I am holy.
When I feel weak, teach me that I am strong.
When I am shattered, assure me that I can heal.
When I am weary, renew my spirit.
When I am lost, show me that You are near.
Amen.

EIGHT

Prayers for Special Occasions

When we are fortunate enough to take part in a joyous event, we sometimes forget to recognize the sanctity of the moment. By the simple act of reciting a prayer, we can turn a happy occasion into a holy one. Too often we assume that we alone are responsible for our good fortune. Offering up a prayer in a time of joy teaches us humility and reminds us that all our gifts come from God.

As a society we spend far too much time and money preparing for the externals of a celebration: the food, the decorations, the attire, the music. We often spend too little time preparing for the *content* of a celebration, for taking stock, for affirming life, for giving thanks. As a result, we are often left with hollow, empty occasions that lack purpose and significance. Uttering a prayer can infuse us with gratitude. Suddenly we become aware of how truly blessed we are. I hope these prayers can help lend sanctity and meaning to moments of joy.

A Graduation Blessing

May all your learning lead to wisdom,
May all your labors lead to success,
May all your knowledge lead you to kindness,
May the path before you lead to blessings,
May your studies never cease,
May all your prayers be answered. Amen.

A Traveling Prayer

Bless my journey, God. Keep me safe from all harm. Open my eyes to the majesty of Your world. Be with me, God, wherever the road may lead. Show me Your wonders; quiet my fears. And when my journey comes to an end, bless my return. Amen.

A New Year's Prayer

I'm good at making resolutions, God. But I'm not very good at keeping them. There are so many goals I'd like to achieve, so many changes I'd like to make.

I pray to You tonight, God, for strength. I want to live a meaningful life, God. I want to comprehend my true promise. I want to understand why You have put me here.

Help me to see, God. Show me the person I have the potential to become. Let me find my passion, God. Teach me to resist temptation, to conquer self-destructive habits, to overcome selfishness and pettiness. Give me the humility and the courage to repair relationships that pride has destroyed. Show me how I can bring hope and healing into this world.

Let this be a good year, God. A year of health, a year of blessing, a year of love, a year of peace. Amen.

A New Home

When I became pregnant with my daughter, my husband, Rob, and I began to search for our first home. We found a real estate agent and started making the rounds at scores of open houses. We both assumed that we would be in our new home by the time the baby came. Things didn't work out that way, however. Homes we liked were out of our price range. The ones we could afford always had a reason for their low asking price. The foundation was cracked on one, another suffered from termite damage, a third had a floor plan that looked like a rat maze, a fourth had such low ceilings that my husband, who is 6'2", kept banging his head on the door frames. We finally did find a nice house that we made an offer on and were about to purchase—when God intervened. It rained in Southern California. When we stopped by to take a final look at the house, water was literally pouring down from just about every ceiling. So much for that one.

Months passed. Before we knew it I was in the hospital in labor and still we had no hopes for a home. I gave birth to our daughter, and now there were four of us in our small apartment.

When my daughter was two weeks old, we began our search again in earnest. Our real estate agent took us to several houses, but none was even worth looking at. Then our agent said that she had one more house for us to see. She suggested that we drive by to look at the exterior. I wasn't very optimistic. Tired and sleep deprived, I lay down across the backseat and told Rob that I didn't want to look at one more house. He parked in front of the place, got out, and didn't return for some time. Then he came back to the car and said, "Nomi, I think you're going to want to see this one." The moment I stepped inside I knew this was my home. The space felt holy to me. It had a deeply spiritual atmosphere. I felt God's presence in the air. We bought the house and moved in shortly thereafter.

On the day the movers came to deliver the furniture, our new next-door neighbor stopped by to introduce herself and to welcome us to the neighborhood. "It's so nice to have a rabbi moving in," she said. "You know who used to live here, don't you?" She went on to tell us about the day the police raided the house and found it full of prostitutes and illicit drugs. I guess my holiness meter was a bit out of whack.

A house is a piece of real estate, an investment. A home is a place that embodies comfort and love and shelter. Taking the time to offer up a prayer can help us transform a house into a home. Decorating tips and construction plans become secondary. Suddenly the structure takes on an air of holiness. It becomes a dwelling place for human beings and for God's presence.

A Prayer for a New Home

Bless this home, God. May it be a shelter of peace, a joyous gathering place for family and friends. May its strength and beauty comfort us. May kindness, love, and health flourish within its walls.

Help us, God, to live without excess, and without envy. Teach us to take pride in the essential blessings: a roof over our heads, food on our table, heat in winter, light in the dark.

Shield us from all harm, God. You are our true shelter, God, our Refuge, our Comfort, our Home. Amen. ✒

Birthday

Two months ago, when I took my children to the library, I watched a small, pale grey-haired woman hunched and wrinkled with years patiently teaching a woman in her thirties how to read. When I returned with my children the following week, they were there again. The old woman pointed to each word and encouraged as the young woman slowly sounded out syllable after syllable, whispering in a timid, embarrassed voice.

Week after week I'd find them sitting there at a low table in the children's section, reading picture books amidst puppets and posters.

Last week when I came to the library, the two women were there working. But this time the young woman held her little boy on her lap. In a calm, confident voice she read to him from *Goodnight Moon*. He listened with rapt attention. The old woman looked on in delight. A mother's shame had turned to pride.

Every day we are given the opportunity to remake ourselves and to remake this world. No matter what our age we have the potential to grow and learn and change. No matter what our age, we have the potential to give and teach and enlighten.

Never stop making birthday wishes.

A Birthday Prayer

I am a year older today, God, and my birthday wish is this: Let me keep growing.

I want to grow, God, not only in years but in strength, in wisdom, in love. I want to gain patience, I want to gain compassion and understanding. This year, please help me to realize the potential You have placed inside me.

Thank You, God, for giving me precious life. Amen.

Rest

We live in a culture that denigrates rest. We think that we need to fill every moment with action. Some people have difficulty with even an instant of silence. Some parents fill their children's lives with so many activities that the kids hardly have any time for fun. Technology has only further complicated this mess. Now, because of cell phones, e-mail, and pagers, the borders between work and home have disintegrated. Colleagues can reach us wherever we are. There are people who cannot turn off their cell phones, who cannot hold a conversation with a live human being in front of them without stopping to take a call. Our work always hovers; stress follows us while we walk or drive or even sit in a movie theater.

Having no separation between work and rest is unhealthy for our bodies and for our souls. Constant work leads to a lack of creativity. You can have all the drive in the world, but if you never stop driving, you will never know all the wonders that have flashed by your window. Life becomes a blur. By always looking for ways to improve ourselves, we fail to make time to simply experience ourselves as we are. If we can learn to leave the world of technology behind for just one day each week, we can begin to experience the world in awe.

Too many of us see rest as a form of laziness. Do you feel guilty when you try to rest? Do you start worrying about all the things you should be doing instead of resting? Rest isn't a lazy activity; it is a holy activity. All the great religions know this. Rest is a way for us to step back and appreciate all that we are, all that we have, all that we have yet to offer. When we rest, we make room for the people we love to enter our lives. We can repair relationships, restore bonds, renew our commitments. A day of rest can transform our lives. It can rekindle romance, save a marriage, it can repair our health, revive our creativity, restore our sanity, renew our weary souls.

My mother taught me an important lesson about the Sabbath. She said that you can't wait passively for the Sabbath to arrive. You have to *make* the Sabbath. You have to prepare your body for receiving the Sabbath; you have to bathe and choose Sabbath clothes that make you feel special. You have to prepare your soul; you have to put away the cares of the week and welcome the precious gift of rest. You have to prepare your home for receiving the Sabbath; you have to fix Sabbath food and welcome Sabbath guests. The atmosphere is magically transformed.

Holy rest is an art form. It's not simply the absence of work. It is the presence of all the sacred pleasures you can partake in: a festive meal, family and friends, a good book, a little romance, a walk in nature, a prayer to God.

Whether you follow a specific religious tradition or not, try to take one day out of your week and turn it into a holy day. Free yourself from all the gadgets that enslave you to the world. Breathe deeply, give thanks, show your family members that you love them. Take a nap, read a book, talk to God. Lie on the grass with your child and stare up at the sky; don't do chores, don't race around. Unclench your jaw and shoulders and fists, let your body relax, let your soul be at ease, listen, taste, feel, touch, enjoy your day of holy rest.

A Prayer for the Day of Rest

I long to change the world, but I rarely appreciate things as they are.

I know how to give, but I don't always know how to receive.

I know how to keep busy, but I don't know how to be still.

I talk, but I don't often listen.

I look, but I don't often see.

I yearn to succeed, but I often forget what is truly important.

Teach me, God, to slow down. May my resting revive me.

May it lead me to wisdom, to holiness, to peace, and to You. Amen.

Giving Thanks

Magazines and food programs teach Americans how to prepare the turkey and decorate the table for Thanksgiving. But families are also looking for ways to enhance the spiritual aspects of the day. Many people are comfortable preparing the feast, but they feel awkward offering up words of gratitude to God. They are not active participants in a given faith tradition, and words of prayer do not come easily to them. What follows is a Thanksgiving prayer that can be said as family and friends gather around the table.

A Prayer for the Thanksgiving Feast

For the laughter of the children,
For my own life breath,
For the abundance of food on this table,
For the ones who prepared this sumptuous feast,
For the roof over our heads,
The clothes on our backs,
For our health,
And our wealth of blessings,
For this opportunity to celebrate with family and
    friends,
For the freedom to pray these words
Without fear,
In any language,
In any faith,
In this great country,
Whose landscape is as vast and beautiful as her
    inhabitants.

Thank You, God, for giving us all these. Amen.

Brushes with Death

One Rosh Hashanah, the Jewish new year, when I was a pulpit rabbi, I asked all congregants who had endured a life-threatening situation over the previous year to rise. I was surprised by the loud rustling of seats. I assumed just a few would stand. But soon scores of people were up. They had all stared into the face of death and lived. Some had undergone risky surgeries. Some had survived heart attacks and strokes. Many had lived through car crashes. One person had been caught in the crossfire between rival gangs. Another had been robbed at gunpoint. After spending a moment in silent gratitude, I asked all the people who were standing to join me in a prayer of thanks for the gift of life.

A Prayer of Thanks After Emerging
from a Life-Threatening Situation

There were times when I prayed and received no answer, when I doubted You were near. I thought I would never live to say the words: Thank You, God. But today I proclaim them with all my body and soul.

Thank You, God, for giving me life and for saving my life. Thank You for allowing me to hold on to everyone I adore and to everything I treasure: my life, my loved ones, my hope, my faith. Amen.

NINE

❧

Prayers for the Blessings of Age

Only children look forward to getting older. The rest of us wish we could stop time. But we have no power over the aging process as it unfolds before us and upon us. We can spend a fortune on hair implants and plastic surgery, but these procedures can't make us even one day younger. What we *do* have, though, is the power to choose how we respond to our own aging. We can dread it, or we can embrace all the gifts that our years have to offer.

Growing older can certainly feel like a curse, especially in a society that idolizes youth. Aging inevitably brings with it a series of losses: the loss of employment and identity; the loss of control, of physical strength and health; the loss of friends; the loss of an illusion of invincibility. But aging also bestows a vast array of blessings upon us: the freedom of life without work, the joys of grandchildren and great-grandchildren, the identity as the elder of a family, the perspective on life that can only be gained through years, the awareness of human frailty, the link to the past that elders can offer, the wisdom that comes with age.

We can get older against our will and become frightened, frustrated, and angry, or we can *grow* older and reap all the benefits of age. Growing older means that we actively choose to continue to develop and live and learn and give and teach and help and bless this world.

A Prayer for Aging with Dignity

I don't want to grow old, God, I don't want any part of it. But since I have no power to stop the clock, my prayer is this: Let me age with grace.

Show me the way, God. Be with me. Grant health to my body and clarity to my mind. Give me strength. Help me to overcome my vanity. Teach me to combat self-pity. Don't allow me to become set in my ways. Shield me from isolation and from loneliness.

May the love of my family and friends be my reward for all the struggles of my youth.

Let all the blessings of age emanate from me. Let wisdom flow from my mouth, let compassion flow from my heart, let acts of kindness flow from my arms, let faith flow from my soul, let joy shine forth from my eyes. Amen.

Menopause

We are comforted by God's predictable rhythms. The sound of our breath in and out, the beating of our hearts. The waves crash against the shore and recede, crash and recede. Day after day the sun rises and sets, the moon waxes and wanes. But a woman's monthly cycle inevitably comes to an end. From the time we are young girls hoping for breasts, we have owned this rhythm. It is a bittersweet blessing. In our teens we dread cramps, bloating, and blood. As we become sexually active we hate how our cycle interferes with spontaneity and forces us to worry about contraception.

But as we mature, we realize that our menstrual cycle is a holy gift, a symbol of fruitfulness, of the fertile ground within us. And soon we become pregnant and grow and grow and bring forth new life. Bringing our children into this world is an unimaginable blessing. And even after we stop having children, our menstrual cycle remains as a monthly reminder to us that we are fresh, in our childbearing years, that there is still a river of life flowing through our wombs. When that river runs dry, we feel sad. We miss the blessing of being a life giver.

A Prayer at Menopause

Help me, God, to embrace life's cycle. When my emotions fluctuate, steady me. When my body temperature rises, shade me beneath your cool, comforting shelter. When my spirit falls, lift me up, God; remind me that I am blessed, that I am beautiful, that I am desirable, that I am whole. When I find myself envying younger women, teach me, God, how to rejoice in the joy of others. Open my eyes to the abundant gifts that surround me each day.

I thank You, God, for making me a woman, for the beauty of youth, for the joy of marriage, for the miracle of childbirth, for the blessings of motherhood, for the beauty that comes with age, for the wisdom of my years.

I am comforted by Your predictable rhythms, God. Amen.

Retirement

Retirement is a milestone we should consecrate. A valued colleague has reached the age of retirement after years of dedication, leadership, and creativity. A precious human being has left an indelible imprint on a workplace and on our society. Too often, we allow people to retire quietly without affording them the honor that is due them.

A Retirement Blessing

Thank you for your insight, your guidance,
your companionship, your integrity, and for
all the sacrifices you made.
May God bless the path you take.
May God bless your future labors with success.
May your newly found freedom bring you great
pleasure and deep satisfaction.
May God bless your body with health and your
soul with joy.
May your work here continue to flourish in your
absence.
May you continue to spread your kindness and
wisdom upon us for many years to come.
May God watch over you and shield you from
harm.
May all your prayers be answered. Amen.

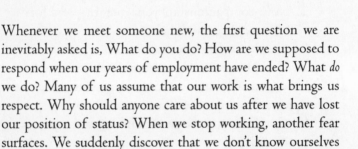 Fear of Retirement

Whenever we meet someone new, the first question we are inevitably asked is, What do you do? How are we supposed to respond when our years of employment have ended? What *do* we do? Many of us assume that our work is what brings us respect. Why should anyone care about us after we have lost our position of status? When we stop working, another fear surfaces. We suddenly discover that we don't know ourselves very well. As children we had interests and passions. But now we are not sure what brings us pleasure. Some of us haven't spent time away from work in years. Even on vacation we were always working in our minds. We aren't sure we know how to enjoy anything anymore.

There is no doubt that retirement is a transition that conjures up many fears. But retirement can also lead to untold joy, to unexpected freedom, to renewed vigor, and to a deeper and truer sense of self-worth.

A Prayer at Retirement

I am scared, God. Who am I without a title? Without a schedule? Without my job? Teach me, God. Show me who I am. Remind me that I am not my job, nor was I ever so.

Open my eyes to the beauty that surrounds me. Open my heart to the love. Open my arms to family members and friends I was always too busy to embrace. Open my mind to the vast world of knowledge that lies before me. Open my ears to the cries of those who desperately need my assistance.

Fill me with compassion, God. Let me transform these doubts of mine into acts of goodness and charity. Calm my fears, God. Remind me that I am vital, that I am needed, that I matter, that I am loved.

Teach me to embrace this precious freedom I have been granted. For the first time in a long time I can choose to spend my days as I wish, to explore whatever I wish, to travel wherever I wish.

Help me live this time wisely, God. Lead me on the path to meaning, to satisfaction, to joy, to peace. Stay with me, God. Let me know You are near. Amen.

The Fear of Becoming Dependent

When we are young, we place our trust in ourselves. But as we grow older our bodies betray us. Our memory mocks us. Our legs weary of carrying us. Our eyes play tricks on us. Our ears won't cooperate. Our hands refuse to obey us. Our stomachs rebel and our looks abandon us. We must learn how to depend upon others. We can laugh about it, but inside we are scared. We are scared of feeling useless. We don't want to become burdens to our children. For years we have taken care of them; now we might have to learn to let them take care of us.

A Prayer When One Fears Becoming Dependent

I don't want to be a burden, God. I certainly don't want pity. But I can no longer do it all alone.

Help me, God. Teach me not to be afraid to rely upon others. Show me how to accept kindness, how to ask for help. Teach me, God, that my children still love me even though they're grown.

I still have so much to offer, God. Help me find the ways to transmit my wisdom, to share my love, to realize my talents, to offer my reassurance and support.

Most of all, I place my trust in You, God; I place my body and soul in Your hands, and pray that You will be with me. Amen.

A Prayer for a Child Who Must Care for an Aging Parent

It's so painful, God, to watch my mother begin to falter. I have always counted on her, and now she needs to count on me. I love my mother; I can't stand the way our roles have reversed. I don't want to see her in her weakness. I know this reversal is humiliating for her. She doesn't want to feel helpless or dependent. But she needs me now.

Help me, God, to rise to this critical occasion. Show me how to care for my mother with respect, tenderness, and love. Fill me with compassion and patience. Shield me from anger and resentment.

Calm my fears, give me strength, God. Help me to seek out relief and support when the burden is great.

Give her strength, God. Bless her with dignity, grace, and health. Amen. ✒

TEN

Prayers of Death and Mourning

When *To Begin Again* was published, I was invited to speak on a television talk show. I felt honored to be offered an opportunity to share my personal and rabbinic experience with so many. I believed that I could offer words of comfort and strength to people who were searching for hope in the midst of sorrow.

One morning, about two weeks before my scheduled appearance, an employee of this show called to pre-interview me. She asked me a series of questions about my book, and I did my best to provide thoughtful answers to her queries. I assumed I was doing a fine job responding to her questions. At one point I was saying, "When someone we love dies, we lose so many—" but she stopped me midsentence and said, "If you continue this way, I'm going to have to bump you off the show." I was stunned. "What am I doing wrong?" I asked. She said, "Don't be depressing. No one wants to feel sad. And don't make people think. People watching this show want to be entertained. They don't want to have to think." Flabbergasted, I said, "Have you read my book? It's about overcoming tragedy." She said, "I'm giving you twenty-four hours to find something upbeat to say. Tell stories. People *like* stories. Remember, nothing depressing, and don't make me think." And she hung up. Now *I* was really depressed.

I spent the rest of the night trying to come up with a happy, peppy way to describe my book about emerging from the depths of sorrow. Eventually I found a way to get my message across by telling a few moving stories. But turning a complex and difficult journey into an inspiring sound bite still feels contrived to me.

The truth is, there is nothing cheerful to say about death. Death is not a story with a happy ending. Death is tragic. It robs us of the people we love. But death is also part of life. We cannot avoid it, and we cannot escape it. Death awaits us as it awaits all those we cherish. Denying our mortality is no comfort. Refusing to talk about loss and mourning does not lead to healing or to uplift; it leads to confusion, isolation, and fear.

After a loved one dies, healing does come. It comes with time and patience and acceptance. It comes when we allow ourselves to feel and express the pain of our loss. There are those who will try to stifle our cries, who will urge us to snap out of our time of sorrow. But the only way I know out of darkness is the path that leads us straight *through* the darkness. Our memories of those we have loved and lost are the beacons that light up our way.

We don't have to sugarcoat our hurts when we appear before God. We don't need to pretend to be strong. God is not afraid of our pain or our anger or our fear. God is our comfort. God is beside us, offering strength and hope and shelter, in life and in death.

What Death Cannot Destroy

Death cannot sever our connection to those we have lost. The soul is eternal and can never be extinguished. But not only the soul survives the grave. The bonds of love are stronger than death. The lessons that our loved ones taught us, their goodness, their deeds, their wisdom will remain with us always. They have left a permanent imprint upon our souls that can never be erased. They continue to guide us wherever we go.

Most people think heaven is a far-off place. But perhaps heaven is closer than we think, perhaps our loved ones are with us. Perhaps they are silently watching over us and sheltering us and guiding our steps. I believe that we are surrounded by the loving presence of those we have loved and lost. May they continue to be with us; may they bless us and inspire us to goodness, in death as they did in life.

A Prayer for Embracing Death

I have so little time, God; help me. I spent years acquiring things, but now I have to learn to travel light. My final journey is here. It's time for letting go. I have been fighting death, denying death, fearing death, but now I must embrace it.

I am frightened. Teach me not to fear, God. Show me how to live each day I have left to the fullest. Open my eyes to the blessings that surround me; open my heart to the love. Give me strength to repair the relationships that have grown cold, the humility to ask for forgiveness, the compassion to forgive.

Let me speak the words I have been too scared to utter. Let me settle affairs I have been unable to face. Let my life be a meaningful legacy to my loved ones and to all those whose lives I have touched. I pray that the love I gave will survive me.

I place my body and soul in Your hands, God. I trust that You will welcome me in love and be with me through the journey to come. Amen.

A Confessional Before Death

I am preparing myself for my departure from this life. Teach me not to fear. Help me, God, to make peace with my approaching death. Stay with me, God; don't leave me. I can't bear the thought of being separated from my loved ones. I will miss this world.

My shortcomings, my wrongdoings, my self-ishness, my lies are all known to You. Forgive me, God, for being less than I could have been, for not always making the best use of the awesome potential You placed inside me.

Please watch over my loved ones, God. Ease their pain, be their comfort. Protect them from harm. Grace them with all that is good. Shelter them with gentleness and love, as I would. Answer their prayers. Grant them health and strength, blessings and joy.

May my life be a source of wisdom to my loved ones and to all those whose lives I have touched. May the love I gave remain with them always, may the lessons I have taught guide them to acts of goodness and honor and compassion. May my memory be a blessing.

I don't know what You have in store for me now, God; I don't know what lies beyond this world. But I believe my soul is eternal and will return to You. I hope You will welcome me in love. I hope to be reunited with loved ones I have lost and to watch over those I must now leave. I place my body and soul in Your hands, God, and pray that You will be beside me through this next journey. Amen.

A Prayer When a Parent Dies

I miss you. You gave me my life. You were my protector, my teacher, my moral compass, my comfort. I feel so alone without you. No one worries about me the way you did. No one loves me the way you did.

Please forgive me for the times I caused you pain, and for the times I took you for granted. I can't begin to fathom all the sacrifices you made for my sake.

I want to thank you for all the ways you blessed my life. Nothing can replace the gaping hole your death has left in my life. But mixed together with all my sadness, there is a great joy for having known you.

I will remember your smile, your touch. I will remember your laughter, your kindness, your generosity, your determination, your love.

Thank you for the time we shared, for the love you gave, for the wisdom you spread. I will always treasure the lessons you taught me. I will carry them with me all the days of my life. I am so proud to be your child.

May God watch over you and bless you, with gentleness and with love. As you blessed me. Rest in peace. Amen.

A Prayer When Mourning a Parent
Who Was Emotionally Unavailable

I missed you when you were alive. I missed the words you never spoke, the affection you didn't give, the apology you wouldn't make. I missed the relationship we never had, the acceptance you couldn't offer.

I've spent my whole life missing you, longing for the parent you could never be. And now that you are gone I miss you even more. I don't want to stop hoping for you to change. I don't want to stop waiting for you. It's hard to let you go, to concede that things between us will never improve.

I love you. And though you weren't able to express it, I believe you loved me too.

May God be with you and bless you with peace. Amen.

A Prayer of Grieving over a Spouse

I miss you every day. I miss your smile and your company and the way you held my hand. I miss the smell of your hair on my pillow and the sound of your voice. I miss our conversations and even our arguments. I miss taking care of you. Of holding you in my arms so tight that you almost seemed like part of me.

The best part of me is gone. It's like a limb that's been amputated, and I keep reaching out to touch it, but all I feel is the cold air rushing between my fingers. And it hurts so much.

But death cannot extinguish your memory, my love. I thank God for the life we shared. I will always treasure our days together. Your abiding love is my blessing and my comfort.

May God take care of you and watch over you, with gentleness and with love, as you took care of me. May God guard you and protect you until that day when I at last find myself beside you once more. Amen.

A Prayer When a Parent Loses a Child

It hurts too much, God. I can't bear it. I don't know how to go on, how to make it through each day. I want to scream. I don't know how to fit in, how to mourn politely and gracefully. People keep telling me I am strong. But I'm not strong. There's nothing left of me. The best of me is dead.

Everything I do feels false. Every conversation is empty and forced. My face is a doll's face, my eyes are glass, my smile is painted on, I keep repeating myself—why? why? why? My arms and legs are lead. My heart is in ruins. I remember a time of laughter and love and music and hope. But death came and destroyed all that, and left me a ravaged survivor.

Help me, God. Give me strength. Ease my suffering. Show me how to live in this world when my soul lies in the grave. Heal my heart, God; be my comfort. Revive my hope, God; teach me to believe that I will come to know blessings and joy once more. Stay with me, God; don't leave me.

Hear my prayer, God. I entrust my child to You, God. Take care of him. Watch over him. Protect him. Spread Your peace over him. Shelter him with gentleness and love. As I would. Guard him until the day when I find myself beside him once more.

Hear me, God. Heal me, God. Amen. ✒

A Prayer When a Loved One Dies by Suicide

Why, God? Why did he have to take his life? Why couldn't I help him? Why couldn't he hold on? Why didn't You save him? Why?

How, God? How will I recover from this nightmare? How can I exorcise the guilt: "I could have done more," "I should have done more," "If only I had . . ." How do I forgive myself? How do I forgive him?

Help me, God. Give me strength to carry on. Heal my anger and shame. Ease the burden on my heart. Teach me to believe that I am not to blame. Lead me back to life and hope and joy.

I know the pain became too much for him. Death was his only hope for release from his suffering. Life offered him no such promise, no relief.

Let him rest now, God. Free from all that haunted him. At peace, at last. Watch over him, God. Be his comfort. Grant him the serenity that he so longed for in life. Let his death be his healing. Amen. ✸

A Prayer When a Loved One Dies
After a Long and Painful Illness

I miss you. I am lonely without you. I am devastated that you were taken from me. I am angry that you had to suffer so. It was so hard to see you in your torment and pain. But that's not how I will remember you.

I will always remember you full of life and warmth and kindness. I will remember the laughter and the love. I will remember the precious time we shared. I will remember your vitality and your grace.

Your death has left a gaping hole in my life. But as hard as it is to be without you, I take comfort in the knowledge that you are at last at peace and free of pain.

Rest in peace. God bless you. Amen.

Losing a Loved One to Violence

Last year, I spoke at a conference sponsored by the Harvard School of Public Health dedicated to healing the violence in our society. As I entered the symposium I looked around and saw people of all faiths and races. They had gathered together from all across the country. And they all had one thing in common. Everyone in the room, including me, had lost a loved one to senseless bloodshed. To an onlooker we must have appeared as a group of utterly dissimilar individuals. But as I sat in my seat beside total strangers, I felt an overwhelming bond. Our pain was shared; our shattered hearts were understood.

A young man whose sister was shot to death in her high school classroom told us that people were so understanding and compassionate at first. But six months later, as his mourning persisted, his coworkers were growing impatient with him. They told him, "Snap out of it, get over it. Get back to your life."

When you first experience a tragedy, you may find an unexpected community of support. It is a blessing. Lean on those who offer their shoulders. Accept their comfort. It will sustain you through the horror and the shock. Unfortunately, at a certain point, most of the people around you eventually must return to the routine of their lives. But you have no such luxury. Your life is in ruins. Unfortunately, your community's departure often happens to coincide with the darkest point of your suffering.

When you first suffer a loss, there is a sense of unreality that surrounds you. You feel numb, in shock; you keep thinking that you will wake up from this nightmare. But in time— it may take weeks or months—the shock gives way to the devastating reality: Your loved one is never coming home again. The newspapers are already focused on the next headlines, the television reporters are camped out at the site of the next trauma, and your community assumes that your pain must have diminished by now. And that is when the real hero's journey begins. The journey that you must take without fanfare, without the outpouring of support. The road that has no markers and no map. The path that will lead you back to life, back to hope, back to strength.

My address to the group lasted forty-five minutes. When I finished speaking, a woman in her late thirties stood up. Her face was drawn. She looked at me and asked in a soft, broken voice, "Do I have to forgive the man who killed my son?" Everyone froze in their seats. I took a deep breath.

This was no ordinary question for me to answer. It was a question loaded with my own pain and loss. When I was a teenager, my father was murdered by a mugger who was never caught. I have often thought about what kind of punishment I would wish upon this anonymous person who stole my father's life and shattered my family. But I have a hard time conjuring up any feelings of hatred toward a man who remains nameless and faceless. At the same time I have no desire to forgive this person who never suffered the consequences of his crime and who never sought forgiveness from my family for his actions. In any case, we are not the ones he ought to be seeking forgiveness from. The one person who could grant him forgiveness lies buried in the ground.

As I looked into the eyes of the suffering childless mother, I thought about my own loss and I replied, "Personally, I'm not that big on forgiveness." Suddenly, people all around the room began to cry. I continued, "If a person commits murder and does not repent, why should I feel compelled to forgive him?" Soon people encircled me. They said this was the first time anyone had ever given them permission not to forgive the murderers. They described it as an enormous cleansing, a release, a healing.

If mourners are moved to forgive a murderer, they should, of course, do so. We should never discourage anyone from offering forgiveness. But I think our society does a great disservice to mourners by telling them that they *must* forgive murderers who demonstrate no remorse. The implicit message to the mourner is: "You don't have enough goodness in your heart if you do not forgive. You haven't mourned correctly if you haven't risen to the level of forgiveness." This pressure to forgive only adds to the suffering of individuals whose hearts are already burdened with untold pain.

A Prayer When a Loved One's Life Is Cut Short by Tragedy

I can't believe I will never see your sweet face again. I am shattered. I keep thinking I'll wake up from this cruel nightmare. But day after day I find myself alone with my pain and my tears.

I wish I could make sense of the senselessness of your death. I wish I could understand God's silence. I wish I could have done something to save you, to protect you from harm. I feel so helpless and so alone.

I pray that you are at peace now, far away from this world's horror. Your life ended in tragedy, but that's not how I will remember you. I will remember your smile, your wisdom, your touch. I will remember your laughter, your kindness, your generosity, your determination, your love.

I know that you wouldn't want me to sink into despair. You always taught me to live up to the best in myself. And that's what I will try to do. I will strive to search for the goodness in every soul, and to live up to the goodness inside my own soul.

Your life was extinguished, but your light can never be extinguished. It continues to shine upon me even in the darkest nights and illuminates my way. You are with me always.

May God watch over you and bless you with peace and eternal love. Amen.

A Prayer for Strength

When I am lost, help me, God, to find my way.

When I am hurt, shelter me with Your loving presence.

When my faith falters, show me that You are near.

When I cry out against You, accept my protest, God, as a prayer too. As a call for You to rid this world of all pain and tragedy.

Until that day, give me the will to rebuild my life in spite of my suffering.

To choose life even in the face of death. Amen.

A Prayer for the Comfort of Memory

God, what I fear most is forgetting him. I've already lost his presence in my life, I can't bear the thought of losing his presence in my mind, my heart, and my soul.

I want to remember it all. His touch, his smell, the look in his eyes. Our conversations, our silences, even our disagreements. I want to remember him as he was without turning him into some kind of saint. I loved him in all his complexity, in all his imperfection.

Help me to remember, God. As I make my way through my busy and sometimes lonely days, may thoughts of him lead me back to times of smiles and laughter. Let my tears and pain be eased by the comfort of his memory.

I will carry the lessons he taught me always. I will try my best to live up to the example he set for me.

Send me strength, God, and comfort, now and always. Amen.

September 11, 2001

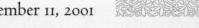

Tuesday, September 11, 2001. The blow was sudden, swift, and beyond comprehension. How can you witness the loss of so many innocent lives and make any sense of it? We can all understand the pain of a single death. That's why the television anchors and newspaper columnists sought to reveal individual stories of heroism and grief to us. Each isolated account brought a sense of reality to the tragedy. But who can grasp the simultaneous horrific deaths of so many without seeing a blur? Who can look into a mass grave and experience the true depth of each life lost?

God can.

There is a blessing Jews are instructed to say when they see a large crowd gathered: "Blessed is God, the Knower of secrets." When we look at a crowd, all we see is a bunch of anonymous people, but when God looks into a crowd, God sees inside each and every soul. God knows us intimately. God knows our goodness, our specialness, our loves, our dreams, our imperfections, our secrets. When three thousand people are murdered together, God bears the loss of each man, woman, and child in his or her uniqueness. God gathers up their pure, innocent souls, and fills them with the peace that was stolen from them on earth. God knows the pain of every single mourner left behind. God weeps with them, and God breathes strength and comfort into their souls.

That is why so many of us began to pray again after September 11. We erected handmade shrines on city streets. We joined together in houses of worship and in sports stadiums to talk to God. At baseball games the traditional seventh-inning-stretch rendition of "Take Me Out to the Ball Game" was replaced by "God Bless America"—a hope, a prayer.

The terrorist attacks of September 11 shook us to the core. We learned that America is more vulnerable than we ever imagined, and we witnessed how fleeting human life is, how fragile. But through our prayers we gained strength. As we turned to God in pain, I believe God's message to every one of us was: You are much stronger than you ever imagined. You are capable of more than you know. You can heal. You can rise above your grief and fear and repair this world. You are capable of acts of goodness that you never knew were inside you.

I believe this was God's message to America too: You are far stronger than you can possibly imagine. Your firefighters, police officers, and soldiers are more heroic than you ever suspected. Your citizens are more courageous and compassionate than you ever guessed. Your suffering will heal; your prosperity will return; you will restore your security and rebuild your ruins; you will live in peace.

And we continue to pray. We pray for a world without hatred, and we pray for an end to terror. We pray for the strength to overcome prejudice and intolerance and for safety and protection. We pray that God will grant wisdom and compassion to our leaders. We pray for our dead and for those left behind. We pray for healing. We pray for ourselves and for this world. We pray for peace.

A Prayer of Remembrance for Fallen Heroes

Some might have stood by, but you stood up. You gave your lives so that others might live. We are indebted to you, we are humbled by you.

When all hope was lost, when the world seemed like a dark and heartless place, you restored our faith in people and our trust in God. You taught us hope, and fearlessness, and honor.

We miss you. We will never forget your heroism. We will teach our children and grandchildren about your courage in the face of danger. We will try with all our might to live up to the example you have set.

We will not ignore human suffering, we will not be indifferent to the cries of those in pain; you did not die in vain. You have changed us. You live on inside us, in pride and in love.

May God watch over you as you watched over us. Rest in peace. Amen.

 Lighting a Candle

It is a Jewish custom to light a memorial candle year after year on the anniversary of a loved one's death. The candle burns for twenty-four hours and is a reminder of the life that was lost and the love that will never die. I recommend this ritual to all those who are searching for a lasting way to sanctify the memory of a loved one.

A Memorial Prayer

I haven't forgotten you, even though it's been some time now since I've seen your face, touched your hand, heard your voice. You are with me all the time.

I used to think you left me. I know better now. You come to me. Sometimes in fleeting moments I feel your presence close by. But I still miss you. And nothing, no person, no joy, no accomplishment, no distraction, not even God, can fill the gaping hole your absence has left in my life.

But mixed together with all my sadness, there is a great joy for having known you. I want to thank you for the time we shared, for the love you gave, for the wisdom you spread.

Thank you for the magnificent moments and for the ordinary ones too. There was beauty in our simplicity. Holiness in our unspectacular days. And I will carry the lessons you taught me always.

Your life has ended, but your light can never be extinguished. It continues to shine upon me even on the darkest nights and illuminates my way.

I light this candle in your honor and in your memory. May God bless you as you have blessed me with love, with grace, and with peace. Amen. ✹

ELEVEN

Prayers for Living Up to the Best in Our Souls

There is a Hasidic story about a wise rabbi named Zusia. When Zusia was on his deathbed he began to cry. His disciple asked him, "Rabbi, why do you weep?" Zusia explained. "When I get to heaven, I won't be troubled if God asks me, 'Zusia, why were you not Abraham?' or 'Zusia, why were you not Moses?' I could answer these questions. After all, I was not endowed with the righteousness of Abraham or the faith of Moses. But what will I say when God asks me, 'Zusia, why were you not Zusia?'"

What will we say when we are asked this question? Why did we fail to fulfill our hope? There is greatness lying dormant inside each and every one of us. There is goodness and generosity and imagination and wisdom. Every human being is endowed with a unique ability to bring a ray of salvation to some corner of this world. Are we living up to our promise? Have we even begun to recognize the awesome light that resides within us? There are no doubt a host of obstacles that block our way. There are external barriers, but there are also internal impediments that prevent us from hearing the call of our souls. Few of us are saints and most of us will never reach the heights we aspire to. But that should never prevent us from striving to be better.

A Prayer for Living Up to the Best in Our Souls

You have blessed me with many gifts, God, but I know it is my task to realize them. May I never underestimate my potential; may I never lose hope. May I find the strength to strive for better, the courage to be different, the energy to give all that I have to offer.

Help me, God, to live up to all the goodness that resides within me. Fill me with the humility to learn from others and with the confidence to trust my own instincts.

Thank You, God, for the power to grow. Amen.

Soul-Searching

Most of us are experts at denying our faults. We ignore our shortcomings; we hide from them; we blame others for our own failings. With our blinders safely in place, we make our way through life. But the story always takes a similar turn. When things go wrong, we wonder why we keep making the same mistakes. The answer is simple. Without honesty, without soul-searching, we can never hope to change or grow. If we want to transform the plot of our lives, we have to learn to become experts at facing our faults.

Self-exploration is painful, and it takes time and enormous strength. But just imagine yourself freed from self-defeating patterns. Imagine yourself responding differently to situations that always tripped you up in the past. Imagine yourself refraining from behaviors that are selfish, cruel, and unworthy of you. Imagine yourself coming closer to the goodness you aspire to.

A Prayer for Facing Our Faults

I have been hiding from my faults, God. I've been blaming others for my own mistakes. Help me, God, to search my soul. Teach me to be honest with myself. Give me the courage to accept responsibility for my actions. Grant me the humility to ask for forgiveness from those I have injured.

Fill me with the desire to change, God. Remind me that I have the power to remake my life. You have filled me with enormous potential, God; teach me how to realize all the gifts of my soul.

Be my guide, God; lead me to goodness, to joy, to learning, and to peace. Amen.

Gossip

There is a Hasidic story about a woman who comes to her rabbi and confesses that she gossiped about a friend. The woman asks her rabbi how she can repair the damage she has caused. The wise and enigmatic rabbi instructs her to take a feather pillow into the marketplace and tear it open. The woman follows the rabbi's directions and returns the following day. She says, "Rabbi, I did what you asked me to do." "Good," replies the rabbi. "Now I want you to take the pillowcase back to the marketplace and retrieve all the feathers." The woman responds, "But Rabbi, the feathers are scattered everywhere; the wind blew them away. I can't possibly get them back." "So now you understand the trouble with gossip," the rabbi explains. "Once you let it loose, there is no way to take it back."

We are all guilty of gossip. We spread it, we listen to it eagerly. The media feeds upon our insatiable appetite for "news" about the private lives of famous people. But gossip is destructive, it hurts, it is petty and not worthy of us.

A Prayer to Abstain from Gossip

Help me, God, to control my mouth. I can't seem to hold a simple conversation without descending into gossip. Sharing my opinions about others, judging them, picking them apart, divulging their secrets has become a pastime for me.

I'm tired of it, God. I want to stop taking pleasure in cruelty. I shouldn't enjoy invading any person's privacy, even when it is a famous person. It's truly none of my business. I hate to imagine what people say about me. I have got to stop.

Give me strength, God. When a piece of scandalous information is on my tongue, teach me to close my lips. When friends entice me with rumors, show me how to discourage their words without seeming superior. If I should slip and spill some bit of gossip, help me to regain control and to repair the damage I have done.

My words have caused far too much pain. Remind me, God, that my words can cause joy. My words can praise, enlighten, encourage, inspire. My words can comfort; my words can heal.

Place wisdom on my lips, God, blessings on my tongue, honor in my heart. Amen.

Overcoming Jealousy

Once a genie told a man he would grant him three wishes. The only drawback was that his neighbor would receive two of whatever he wished for. So first the man wished for a Rolls-Royce, and he was exuberant until he noticed that his neighbor had two Rolls-Royces. Then he wished for a mansion, and he was overjoyed until he looked across the street and saw that his neighbor had two mansions. Finally, for his last wish the man said, "Genie, I wish to be blind in one eye."

When jealousy takes root within us, it poisons our relationships and our souls. It prevents us from appreciating our blessings because we are forever coveting other people's advantages. When we are jealous, our vision becomes so distorted that we can take no joy in what is ours.

A Prayer to Combat Jealousy

Why do I keep comparing myself to others? Why do the successes of my friends cause me pain? Why can't I be satisfied with the life I have?

I'm tired of not measuring up, God. I'm tired of praying for my rivals to fail. I'm tired of having rivals at all.

Teach me, God, to treasure my life. Give me the strength to overcome my jealousy. Show me how to take pleasure in my life. Help me to rejoice in the joy of others, to wish them nothing but blessings.

Soften my heart, God; open my eyes to all the gifts that surround me. Let me find peace, God.

Thank You, God, for all that you have given me. Amen.

A Prayer for Restraining One's Temper

I am too quick to anger, God. I need to learn how to control my temper. In my rage I have said hurtful things that I deeply regret. And there is no way to erase the hateful words I have spoken. I cause pain to those I love. I constantly sabotage myself.

Help me, God. I am ashamed of my behavior. Teach me how to master my rage. Show me how to breathe deeply, how to find calm.

Lead me, God, to patience and restraint. Remind me that I have the power to contain my fury. Help me to see that there is a way to express anger with dignity and grace. Help me to believe that I can change. Fill me with the humility, God, to seek forgiveness from those I have hurt.

Soften my heart, God; fill me with Your comfort. Guide me on the path to goodness, to compassion, to love, to honor, and to peace. Amen. ⚑

A Prayer for Overcoming Indifference

I watch the news, God. I observe it all from a comfortable distance. I see people suffering, and I don't lift a finger to help them. I condemn injustice, but I do nothing to fight against it. I am pained by the faces of starving innocent children, but I am not moved enough to try to save them. I step over homeless people in the street, I walk past outstretched hands, I avert my eyes, I close my heart.

Forgive me, God, for remaining aloof while others are in need of my assistance.

Wake me up, God; ignite my passion, fill me with outrage. Remind me that I am responsible for Your world. Don't allow me to stand idly by. Inspire me to act. Teach me to believe that I can repair some corner of this world.

When I despair, fill me with hope. When I doubt my strength, fill me with faith. When I am weary, renew my spirit. When I lose direction, show me the way back to meaning, back to compassion, back to You. Amen.

A Prayer to End Procrastination

I am a procrastinator, God. My work piles up, my obligations mount, and my anxieties overwhelm me. I mean to change, but I keep falling back into old patterns. I let my colleagues down, I disappoint my friends, I hurt myself.

Help me, God. Give me the strength to bring order into my life. Fill me with the ability to respond quickly to any task I must complete. Teach me to face down my fears, God. Remind me that putting off responsibilities is always more painful than confronting them head-on.

I live as if I have all the time in the world to accomplish my goals. I say to myself, this can wait until tomorrow. But the truth is, You have given me only limited time on this earth.

Inspire me, God, to remake myself. Be my guide, God; lead me to achievement, to fulfillment, to deep satisfaction, and to peace. Amen.

A Prayer to Overcome Vanity

I spend too much time looking in the mirror, God, and not enough time looking in my soul. I worry more about how I appear each day than I do about how I behave. I squander money on myself that I could be spending to assist others. Show me, God, how to see beyond myself to those who are waiting for my help. Give me the strength to overcome my vanity. Teach me how to change. Let me devote my time to realizing all the potential that lies within me. Let me learn and grow and bless this world. Remind me, God, that grace, the deepest beauty of all, emanates from the soul. Amen. ✒

A Prayer When We Are Too Hard on Ourselves

Teach me how to love myself, God. I am so critical of myself. I set such high standards for myself. I accept shortcomings in others, but I am so unforgiving of myself. Help me, God. Teach me how to enjoy my life. Remind me to be kind to myself. Show me how to embrace the person I am. Lead me to appreciate all the miracles that surround me each day. Soften my heart, God; open my eyes. Fill me with the capacity to treasure my life. Thank You, God, for creating me as I am. Amen. ✒

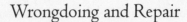

We all make mistakes. We lie, we betray friends, we hurt those we love. We are selfish, we envy others, we are self-righteous and unforgiving. We are fallible. We are human. But acknowledging our imperfection doesn't absolve us of responsibility. There is no excuse for not trying to live up to the best in ourselves. Being human means that we are capable of reflection, of introspection, of regret, of contrition. Being human means that we are capable of change and of growth. We can repair what we have shattered; we can seek to heal what we have broken; we can do everything in our power to revive what we have destroyed.

God has faith in us; God knows the goodness that lies dormant within us. The question is, do we have the courage to live up to our highest potential?

A Prayer After Wrongdoing

I wish I could take it back, God. I wish I could turn back the clock and do it all differently. This time I would listen to my conscience. This time I would think before I acted. This time I would pray for Your guidance.

But I can't erase the past. All I can do is regret the choice I made. I was selfish. Now I will have to suffer the consequences of my actions.

Give me the courage, God, to admit I was wrong and apologize. I will have to find a way to repair the damage I have done. I will have to learn to act with integrity, compassion, and honor.

Forgive me, God, for not living up to the best in myself. Give me strength to endure my guilt and humiliation.

You have blessed me with so many gifts, God; help me to realize them. Please don't leave me, God; don't give up on me, be with me. Let me know You are near. Amen.

Healing Troubled Relationships

What will the messianic era look like? Will the lion lie down with the lamb? Will the dead be resurrected? My favorite account of the time to come is found in the Book of Malachi: "Behold, I will send you Elijah the Prophet . . . And he will turn the hearts of parents to their children and the hearts of children to their parents." It's a simple vision of a perfected world. There are no astonishing supernatural upheavals. But the transformation is no less astounding. The locus of change is the human heart, in the love between parents and children. Imagine a time when families are free from friction and hostility, when relationships that have grown cold are revived, when loved ones who refuse to talk to each other suddenly reunite and embrace. Paradise unfolds in small increments. Peace in the heart will bring peace in the family. Peace in the family will bring peace at work. Peace at work will bring peace in society. Peace in society will bring peace in the world. That is the messianic era.

Do we need to wait for Elijah to repair relationships that we ourselves have the power to mend? Peace begins when we find the courage to soften our hardened hearts.

A Prayer for the Strength to Heal a Troubled Relationship

I've been stubborn, God, and unforgiving. I love my son, God. I miss him. I've let pride tear us apart. I hardened my heart against him. But my heart still longs for him.

I want to tell him I'm sorry for all the pain I've caused. I want to embrace him. But I'm frightened. I'm scared he'll turn away from me. The truth is, I don't trust myself. I'm worried that I'll say the wrong words, that we'll just end up in another argument.

How do you wipe away years of hostility? How can you erase the resentment, the bitterness, the hurt? Where do you begin?

Be my guide, God. Send me the right words to speak. Show me that I am capable of more than this mess I have created. Teach me to replace my self-righteousness with humility, my temper with compassion, my brooding with forgiveness. Soften my heart, God; open my arms.

I know that I cannot erase years of friction in a single grand gesture. I will have to earn his trust. I will have to learn to truly hear his complaints. I will have to change.

Grace me with patience, God. Teach me perseverance. Fill me with resilience, with hope, with abiding love. Amen.

The Strength to Forgive

Earlier, when discussing an unrepentant murderer, I said, "I'm not that big on forgiveness." But I am very big on forgiveness when someone honestly seeks to remake his or her life and repair the damage he or she has done. Often we maintain our anger as a shield against pain. But holding on to anger or a desire for vengeance doesn't prevent us from getting hurt. By hardening our hearts we hurt ourselves. We preclude the possibility of reviving a relationship that can in fact be resurrected.

When a friend offers up a sincere apology, when a loved one takes responsibility for his or her actions and expresses an honest desire to change and to heal the pain he or she has caused, may we find the strength in our hearts to forgive. May we work together to mend the bonds that have been torn.

A Prayer for the Strength to Forgive

Someone close to me hurt me. I have good reason to be angry. I want him to suffer for the pain he caused me. But how long should I hold on to my anger? I can see now that by hardening my heart I am punishing myself as much as him.

Soften my heart, God; teach me compassion. Show me how to accept his apology, how to forgive him, how to trust him once more.

Help us repair our relationship, God. Heal our pain. Help us to wipe away the resentments and the hurt.

Restore us, God, to the way we were before. Lead us back to laughter, to kindness, and to love. Amen.

Shelter

We spend a lot of time trying to uncover people. Newspapers disclose facts about the private lives of public figures. Gossip columns strip them bare. We go into therapy and dissect our loved ones to pieces. We pick our friends apart behind their backs. We watch talk shows that encourage people to bare their souls to millions of onlookers. We want to know.

There are certainly situations when it is crucial to reveal the truth about someone. But is there no room for shelter?

Most children learn about Noah in Sunday school. He is the man who built the ark and filled it with the animals two by two. But most of us never learned about what happened to Noah after the flood. Noah plants a vineyard, gets drunk, and exposes himself. His youngest son walks in on his father in his state of shame and runs to spread the news to his older brothers. But the brothers walk into their father's tent backward and avert their eyes so as not to look upon their father in his nakedness. They spread out a cloak and cover him up in compassion and respect.

What would happen if, instead of trying to expose people, we tried to cover them up? What if, instead of searching for their flaws, we tried to overlook their shortcomings?

What if we were to embrace our loved ones with all their faults and imperfections? What if we refused to listen to reports that invade people's privacy? Our world desperately needs an infusion of compassion. We all pray that God will shelter us and not judge us too harshly. Can't we learn to offer this same kindness to each other?

A Prayer for Offering Compassion

I can sometimes be very critical, God. I pass judgment on people I don't even know. I fixate on the faults of my loved ones instead of focusing on their strengths.

Help me, God, to learn the way of compassion. When someone is exposed, let me be a shelter. When someone is vulnerable, teach me to offer protection.

Bless my eyes, God; show me how to uncover the goodness in others and overlook their shortcomings. Teach me to embrace people with all their imperfections. That is, after all, how I hope they will approach me.

Inspire me, God, with the gift of grace. Bless me and shelter me in Your compassion and love. Amen. ✍

A Prayer for Meaning and Satisfaction

I have an insatiable appetite, God. It feels like there is an emptiness inside me that can never be filled. I keep wanting more—more money, more possessions, more success. But no matter what I do, a hunger still remains. I feel uneasy, God. I am agitated.

Help me, God. Help me to see that I can't fill this void with distractions or new possessions. My soul is crying out for meaning. Teach me how to nourish my soul, God. Show me how to find fulfillment.

I want my life to matter, God. I want to uncover my passion. I want to know why You put me here.

Be with me, God; lead me on the path to blessings, to joy, to deep satisfaction, and to peace. Amen.

A Difficult Decision

Should I work to save my marriage, or is it time for me to leave? Should I place my father in a convalescent home, or should I try to care for him myself? Should I remain in this job and try to make it work, or should I quit and search for a new direction? Should I say yes and marry this person, or should I say no and move on?

There comes a time in each of our lives when we are faced with a difficult decision.

A Prayer for Wisdom and Guidance

God, I need to make an important decision, and I don't know which way to turn. I feel ambivalent and insecure. I wish I had eyes to peer into the future to know which path is the correct one.

Help me, God. Send me Your guidance. Fill me with the insight to choose wisely. Remind me not to panic; remind me to take the time I need to make an informed decision. Teach me how to properly weigh each option. Give me the courage to trust my instincts, the faith to trust my intuition.

Be with me, God; lead me on the path to blessings, to joy, and to peace. Amen.

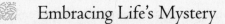 Embracing Life's Mystery

In my family, there is a strange mystery surrounding the date June 23. My father died on June 23, 1978. Four years later my sister, Mimi, became pregnant and learned that she was due in late June. When she entered her ninth month, her obstetrician told her she was going to need a cesarean section and that she should schedule a date. Mimi didn't want her child to be born on the day our father died, but for some reason she thought he had died on the twenty-first of June, so she chose to have her surgery two days later. After her son Jared was born, my sister was shocked to learn that she had actually given birth on the anniversary of our father's death.

When my mother reached the age of sixty-five, she filled out an application to receive her Social Security benefits. For her date of birth, she put down the date our family has always celebrated: August 25, 1922. But since my mother was born in Poland, the Social Security Administration required that she produce an original copy of her birth certificate. My mother doubted there was any such record of her birth in Poland, but just the same, she wrote to a Polish government agency. A few months later she received a reply. She opened the envelope and pulled out a piece of paper. To her surprise it was her birth certificate. My mother was born on June 23, 1922.

My mother was born, my father died, their first grand-child was born, all on June 23.

Life is full of mysteries we may never fully comprehend. There are times when we feel in control, when we assume we are the authors of our fate, and there are other times when events force us to recognize our smallness and embrace what we cannot begin to fathom. In the biblical Book of Deuteronomy, Moses says, "The hidden things belong to God, but the revealed things belong to us and our children." We may never know God's secrets or God's ways; we may never uncover the key to occurrences that baffle and astound us. Life's unpredictability teaches us humility; life's mysteries teach us reverence and awe.

A Prayer for Embracing Life's Mystery

I want to know You, God. I want to see the world through Your eyes. To feel intimately involved in all of creation. I want to know why things happen the way they do.

Help me, God, to accept what I cannot understand, to accept life without constantly trying to control it. Teach me how to bend with life, how to repair what I can repair, how to live with my questions, how to rejoice in Your wonders.

When I am faced with events that baffle and astound me, help me to transform my frustration into humility and awe. Teach me to embrace the mystery, God. Remind me to enjoy the ride.

Thank You, God, for this spectacular life. Amen. ✍

TWELVE

Prayers for Our Country and Our World

In the story of the Exodus, Moses asks Pharaoh to release the Children of Israel from Egypt, but Pharaoh refuses and soon Moses is forced to bring on the ten plagues. Moses turns the waters of the Nile to blood; then Pharaoh calls upon his sorcerers, who easily duplicate this feat. Moses brings on the plague of frogs, then Pharaoh's sorcerers cause frogs to appear as well. The only difference between the powers of Moses and the powers of the Egyptian sorcerers is this: Only Moses can reverse the plagues. Pharaoh's sorcerers can produce plagues, but they have no power to revoke them.

It takes no talent to bring about a plague, to cause war and pain and disaster. But it takes enormous courage and faith to eradicate a plague, to bring about peace, to cure disease, to triumph over darkness.

Unfortunately, there is no shortage of plagues in our world. Our planet is cursed by war, poverty, disease, injustice, hatred, and pollution. What will we say to our children when they turn to us one day and ask, "Why didn't you do anything to stop this?" Too many of us have been indifferent to the afflictions that surround us.

God has endowed every single one of us with enormous

power. God has entrusted us with this fragile, precious world. We have learned well how to wield our strength to cause tremendous devastation. But God is praying that we will finally learn how to utilize our strength to take full custody of our world; that we will learn well how to produce a time of unprecedented blessing.

A Prayer for a Better World

You have given us a wonderful and horrible world, God. Why? Why is this world so beautiful and majestic and yet so full of disaster and disease? Why is there abundance and dire poverty, kindness and cruelty? Why do some live in peace while others live in fear and war? Why did You bless us with one hand, God, and then curse us with the other?

Please show Yourself, God; help us. Give us the wisdom to eradicate disease, the tools to end hunger, the courage and compassion to overcome hatred and bloodshed. Turn our complacency into action, soften our hardened hearts, transform our despair into hope.

Grace us with Your presence, God; teach us how to bless our world with health, abundance, joy, and peace. Amen. ✒

A Prayer When Our Country Is at War

Men and women have been called to serve our country in this time of war. Watch over them, God, on the ground, in the air, in the heart of the seas. Keep them safe. Bless them with courage and compassion, with wisdom and might, and with Your holy light. Grant them a swift victory, God, over those who threaten our world with tyranny and terror.

Hear their prayers, God. Bring peace. Let it rain down from the heavens like a mighty storm. Let it wash away all hatred and bloodshed.

Please, God. Gather our fallen into Your eternal shelter where there is no hatred, no pain, and no war. Just peace. Amen.

A Prayer for Peace

Let us live in peace, God.
Let children live in peace, in homes free
from brutality and abuse.

Let them go to school in peace, free from violence
and fear.

Let them play in peace, God, in safe parks, in safe
neighborhoods; watch over them.

Let husbands and wives love in peace, in marriages
free from cruelty.

Let men and women go to work in peace, with no
fears of terror or bloodshed.

Let us travel in peace; protect us, God, in the air,
on the seas, along whatever road we take.

Let nations dwell together in peace, without the
threat of war hovering over them.

Help us, God. Teach all people of all races and
faiths, in all the countries all over the world, to
believe that the peace that seems so far off is in
fact within our reach.

Let us all live in peace, God. And let us say,
Amen.

In Nature

It's so easy to be removed from nature. We speed around in our cars and forget what it's like to walk upon the earth. We sit all day in an office untouched by the light of the sun or the shade of an old tree. We lie in our beds at night without seeing the stars or the moon. We turn on our lamps and forget about the mysterious darkness that beckons us to pay attention.

One day I was walking along the beach with my Walkman blasting, unable to hear the crashing waves calling out to me: stop, look, listen, smell. Suddenly I stopped. I sat. The sand felt good against my skin. The smell of salt in the air calmed me; the tide kept rising. Every few minutes I moved farther back on the sand to avoid getting wet. Then I changed my mind. I sat and waited. The water came, and I let it soak me. I screamed in delight; I shivered. The salt tasted good on my tongue and stung my eyes. The sand stuck to me. I felt alive. Seagulls stepped all around me making intricate patterns with their feet. I found a shiny shell painted with all the colors of the rainbow. I sighed a deep sigh. And I prayed.

A Prayer for the Wonders in Nature

Thank You, God,
for the sand and the stars,
for the oceans and the mountains,
for all the living creatures
whose spirits are somehow connected to my own.
Thank You for the forests and the flowers,
for the fertile soil
and the power to grow.
Thank You for life's rhythms,
the seasons and the phases of the moon,
for the sky above me,
and the soul within me.
Thank You, God, for placing me
in a world so vast and majestic.
Everywhere I turn I see a sign
that leads me straight to You. Amen.

Tolerance

I was riding in a taxi in Cleveland on my way to give a lecture about the strength of the human spirit. The cabdriver was very talkative and friendly, and soon he asked, "So what do you do?" I said, "I'm a rabbi." And then there was a dead silence. My response obviously disturbed this man. Perhaps he disapproved of women in the clergy. I didn't know what to think. I waited. After a long pause he spoke: "On behalf of all black people I'd like to apologize to your people for the hateful words of Louis Farrakhan." Then he added, "My father was in the army during World War II. He helped to liberate a concentration camp and saw firsthand what was done to the Jewish people. All my life he taught me to speak out against lies and prejudice because he saw with his own eyes what hatred can lead to." Now I was the one who was taken aback. After a long silence I said to him, "For every person like Louis Farrakhan there are a thousand more like you who restore my faith in human kindness."

Soon we reached my destination. When the cab stopped, the driver got out and came around to where I was standing, and then two people, a black man and a white woman, a Christian and a Jew, two complete strangers, embraced. I spoke that night about my rare encounter inside a taxicab; it was a lecture about the strength of the human spirit.

Why do we fear differences? How can we hate people we don't even know? When God looks at us, God cherishes our differences just as a parent cherishes each child's uniqueness. This one has brown hair and this one is blonde, and I love them both. How much blood has been spilled over differences in hair color, in skin color, in faith? In God's eyes we are one. All of us, all people, all nationalities, all races and religions. Will we ever find a way to see each other through God's eyes? Will we ever embrace our differences? Will we ever look beyond our differences to uncover the sameness that unites us all? In God's eyes we are one.

A Prayer for Tolerance

Teach us, God, to treasure the differences that distinguish one person from another. Fill us with the strength to overcome senseless fear and hatred.

Open our hearts to the radiance that shines forth from every human soul. Inspire us to shed our apathy; remind us that it is our obligation to be responsible for one another.

Open our ears to the cries of all who are in need of our assistance. Give us the courage to combat prejudice and intolerance wherever they exist.

Teach us to see each other through Your eyes, God. In Your eyes all people are equally loved, equally precious.

Bless us all, God, with compassion, with kindness, and with peace. Amen. ✍

 Conclusion

BECOMING A PRAYER

True prayer leads us to action. Dr. Abraham Joshua Heschel was a brilliant theologian and a passionate social activist. When he marched for justice with Dr. Martin Luther King Jr. in Selma, Alabama, he proclaimed, "It felt as if my legs were praying." The goodness we perform in this world is our highest prayer.

When we struggle to repair this world, when we rise above our complacency and offer compassion, charity, and love, we are praying. When we fight to eradicate poverty, injustice, and war, when we take the time to perform acts of kindness, we are praying. When we gather the strength to give of ourselves to those who so desperately need our assistance instead of averting our gaze, we are praying. "I *am* my prayer to You, God," the Psalmist cried out. When our actions embody our soul's deepest yearnings we become a prayer.

SAVING GOD'S LIFE

A sage once wrote that whenever we reach out to help someone who is suffering, God speaks words of gratitude to us.

God says, "Thank you for saving My life." What does this mean? Why would God say these words? Isn't God immortal? How can any person save God's life? I'll explain:

When a poor mother lives on the streets with her children, she cries out day after day, "Help me, God. Save me. Lift me and my children out of hunger and homelessness." And when no help comes, when she watches people walk by her without even glancing her way, she lowers her head to the ground and says to herself, "There is no God. God is dead."

But when someone draws near and provides solace and support, she turns her face up to the heavens and whispers, "Thank You, God."

Whenever we rise above our indifference and complacency, whenever we refuse to ignore cries of suffering, whenever we make the choice to help any human being in need, we become God's partners. And a sacred voice echoes across the world speaking softly, "Bless you, thank you, for saving My life."

TELL IT TO GOD

A close friend of mine called me just last night and said, "Nomi, I need your help. I want you to teach me how to pray." She told me that whenever she goes to a house of worship she tries to sing along, but she feels nothing. Just words. She said she's been trying to meditate in a quiet spot, hoping for some kind of communication with God, but she feels nothing. Just silence. I said to her, "This problem you're having, tell it to God, and you'll be praying."

There are many forms of prayer we can learn, but the one

we can all start with is the prayer of our souls. We don't have to introduce ourselves to God; God already knows us. We don't have to say anything profound; we don't have to sound smart. God doesn't care. We don't have to be sitting quietly in a state of prayerful devotion; whenever we speak, God listens. We don't have to speak volumes; we don't need to have an agenda; we just need to face God. We can have a running dialogue with God all day long. We can just say a quick hello.

As we enter into an intimate relationship with God, our lives start to open up. Answers start to appear. We begin seeing things we never noticed before. Days that used to feel empty are suddenly infused with meaning. Anxiety gives way to calm, despair gives way to hope, fear gives way to faith, frustration gives way to peace, sadness gives way to joy. Most of all, through prayer our indifference gives way to action.

Prayer reminds us that we are connected through God to one another, to all those longing for our help. Our souls are tied to the souls of all people. Our souls are tied to the souls of all those who have come before us. We are not alone. We are not cut off. We have not been forgotten. God is with us. God has filled us with enormous potential. But God has given us only limited days. God is praying for us. God is hoping we will learn how to take care of one another. The world is waiting for us to bless it.

Each of us has a prayer in our hearts. A prayer of singular importance. Chances are we will find it only by opening our hearts and speaking it directly to God. When the moment is right, close your eyes. Take a deep breath in and, as you breathe out, relax. Without censoring or editing, look inside yourself. Look deep down inside. Find the prayer of your soul. Find it and speak it to God. Tell God your pain, your hope, your joy. Share your deepest longing. Express your anger. Ask for God's help. Tell God your secret. Thank God for your blessings. Shout, sing, whisper, talk to God. And listen closely for a reply.

> *May you receive an answer that will bring you joy and peace. May God be with you, may health and strength sustain you, may nothing harm you, may wisdom and kindness enrich you, may you be a blessing to this world, and may blessings surround you now and always. Amen.*

© JACK BEHR

A NOTE ABOUT THE AUTHOR

Naomi Levy was in the first class to admit women to study for the rab-
binate at the Jewish Theological Seminary of America, and the first female
Conservative rabbi to lead a congregation on the West Coast. Author of
the acclaimed book *To Begin Again*, she lives in Venice, California, with her
husband, Robert Eshman, and their children, Adin and Noa.